"Sandy Swenson's book *Just Dandy* is a wise and intimate portrayal of navigating life's unexpected challenges. With warmth and humor, she reminds us that even when a child's addiction is consuming all our attention, life is often about starting over—and then starting over again. Inspiring!"

—**BEVERLY CONYERS,** author of *Find Your Light* and *Addict in the Family*

"Sandy Swenson is a gifted writer! She knows how to tell a story that holds your interest and keeps you coming back for more. *Just Dandy* is Sandy's story, from her son Joey's addiction to her divorce to her various moves to re-create her new life. Too she is helping her parents through their transition to needing more care. Through it all, Sandy stays strong, putting one foot in front of the other, maneuvering herself through the turmoil. Other moms will relate to all that Sandy is going through—her pain, her resilience, and her efforts to move forward in positive ways."

—**CATHY TAUGHINBAUGH,** Parent Coach,
creator of Regain Your Hope online course

"Sandra Swenson has written a book about the transformation of pain and loss through grace and hard work into a beautiful service to others. She tells her story with candor and humility, including the lessons she learned along the way. Highly recommended!"

—**TIM PORTINGA,** PsyD, LP, Manager of Mental Health and
Family Program at Hazelden Betty Ford Foundation

"While reading *The Joey Song,* I thought, 'This woman has peeked in my windows.' This newest book, *Just Dandy,* shares a deeper look into her life, its struggles and pain. Sandy is a woman whose trials and pain have graced her with strength to become a support for so many!"

—**KIM PALMER,** a fellow mom of an addicted son

"*Just Dandy* is a story of betrayal, recovery, deep grief, profound healing, loss, uncertainty, undying love, unimaginable possibility, and eternal hope all wrapped up in one exquisitely written book. It offers hope that pain isn't forever, pain isn't the end, and pain can be transformed into something beautiful."

—**BARB KLEIN,** author of *111 Invitations: Step into the Full Richness of Life*

"Sandra Swenson nailed it again! *Just Dandy* presents a window into her life story of vulnerability and surviving what feels overwhelming—addiction, divorce, aging parents, empty nesting, loneliness—transforming heartache and loss into purpose and intentional living. It offers a path toward healing and hope for individuals and families living in chaos."

—**ANITA BONT,** LMFT, LADC, Manager of Family Program and Spiritual Care at Hazelden Betty Ford Foundation

"In her fourth publication, *Just Dandy,* Sandy Swenson once again brings her poignant voice to the written word as she chronicles her journey to 'self' and to fulfilling her mission, purpose, and passion to help moms of children with addiction."

—**LISA FREDERIKSEN,** author of *The 10th Anniversary Edition If You Loved Me, You'd Stop!* and founder of BreakingTheCycles.com

"Sandra lets us into her home and her heart. A bold battle cry for moms, wives, and daughters, reminding us that we are not alone. She brings us to a place where love, grief, hope, and heartache meet."

—**KELLY RYAN,** MA, LAADC, Supervisor of the Family Program at Hazelden Betty Ford Foundation

just dandy

*Living with
Heartache and Wishes*

BY SANDRA SWENSON

Hazelden
Publishing

Hazelden Publishing
Center City, Minnesota 55012
hazelden.org/bookstore

Library of Congress Cataloging-in-Publication Data

Swenson, Sandra, 1959– author.

Just dandy : living with heartache and wishes / by Sandra Swenson.

LCCN 2020028985 (print) | LCCN 2020028986 (ebook) |
ISBN 9781616498825 (paperback) | ISBN 9781616498832 (epub)

LCSH: Swenson, Sandra, 1959– | Parents of drug addicts—Biography. |
Adult children of aging parents—Biography. | Happiness.

LCC HV5805.S94 A3 2020 (print) | LCC HV5805.S94 (ebook) |
DDC 362.29/12092 [B]—dc23

LC record available at https://lccn.loc.gov/2020028985

LC ebook record available at https://lccn.loc.gov/2020028986

Editor's notes:

This publication is intended to support personal growth and should not be thought of as a substitute for the advice of health care professionals. The author's advice and viewpoints are her own.

Quotations are taken from Sandra Swenson's books *The Joey Song: A Mother's Story of Her Son's Addiction* (2014, Central Recovery Press), *Tending Dandelions: Honest Meditations for Mothers with Addicted Children* (2017, Hazelden Publishing), and *Readings for Moms of Addicts* mobile app (2018, Hazelden Publishing).

The poem "Everything Falls Away" appears on page 230 with permission of Parker J. Palmer, Madison, Wisconsin.

24 23 22 21 20   1 2 3 4 5 6

Cover design: Theresa Jaeger Gedig
Interior design: Terri Kinne
Typesetting: Bookmobile Design & Digital Publisher Services
Developmental editor: Andrea Lien
Editorial project manager: Jean Cook

This book is dedicated to mamas everywhere.

To my sisters of the heart.

Together we are stronger.

Like a dandelion
      up through the pavement,
I persist.

— WENTWORTH MILLER

CONTENTS

Dear Mamas

NO ONE EVER SAID it was going to be easy, but no one ever said it would be this hard, either. And even if they had, I would never have believed them. *It* being life, with all its unexpected heartache piled atop crumpled dreams and wishes.

As the mom of a now-adult child who battles addiction, I know the devastating toll of this disease—the love and lies, fears and hopes, twisting the mystical umbilical connection into knots. Addiction is ruthless, breaking hearts and bonds and all the rules. Oh, how I wish there were a way to go back in time and nudge the direction of our path over a smidge, just enough to lead us anywhere but here, this place where love and addiction meet. However, as much as I wish my family could have avoided all the pain, trauma, and drama, the truth is I'm a better person now than I was even aware I could be. I have had to dig deep, feel big, see truth, and be real. Because of that, I've discovered a deeper level of patience, acceptance, kindness, and understanding of what really matters. For that, I'm grateful. I'm also grateful, of course, for all the wonderful mamas I've met along the way. The brave, strong, hurt, terrified, confused, open-armed, and open-hearted sisterhood that would otherwise not have blessed my life.

For many years, I was consumed with my son's addiction, thinking I could fix it, change him, or *somehow* manage his life and disease for him. Over time, I came to realize the only thing

I can change or control is *me*—but that has real power. Through my words and actions, I can help shed the shame and stigma, changing the way addiction is perceived within my community and within my son himself. And, through my books, blog, and MomPower website, in trying to help other moms on the same path, I have found healing. But I'm also tired. My sixty-year-old self would like to take a rest, but being the mom of an addicted child is a continuous uphill journey of learning and adapting, while carrying an unrelenting grief for what is, for what should have been, and in anticipation of what might be coming next—in addition to everything else we juggle as mothers, wives, daughters, caregivers, worker bees, and friends. Life is not one-dimensional. There's a lot of other tough stuff piling up, too—day after day, year after year, one after another on top of another.

But, as moms with addicted children, we are strong—my goodness, we continue to endure the unimaginable every single day!—and we have learned more ways to cope than we may even be aware of. Ways to think and see and respond to all the other tough stuff we're faced with, too. We may not be able to make every situation *better*, but we can behave in ways that make them *not worse*. We really can find our way to being *just dandy* (and mean it).

Several years ago, at a museum with my dad, I was drawn to a glass case displaying a partially completed piece of handwoven lace, with the dozens of delicate threads being used in this creation laid out like sunbeams from the center. Attached to the end of each thread was a wooden bobbin, giving, I assume, the weaver something of substance to hold on to while also helping to keep the multitude of threads laid out in some sort of manageable arrangement. I told my dad that the piece-of-lace-in-the-works *looks* like what it *feels* like to write a book—keeping all the individual thought-threads separate and untangled, and keeping track of which one goes where and how to find my way back to pick up at the place I left off. That piece of bobbin lace also looks the same way my life feels: nothing happens in a straight line— neither around me nor within me; sometimes it looks impossible to figure out; it is still incomplete; and it won't look the same at the end as it did at the beginning—but I believe that even life's most chaotic jumble of threads can be woven into something beautiful.

We have the power to thrive, even while living with heartache and wishes.

Hugs and hope,
Sandy

Part One

Bridal Veil Falls

**A tear
carries the weight
of a lifetime.**

—WENDY MURRAY

1

From Point A to Point WTF

I think it's important to realize
we can miss something, but not want it back.

—PAULO COELHO

A BIT OUT OF BREATH, sweaty, and dusty from my hike through the forest up to Bridal Veil Falls, I climb onto a boulder across from the waterfall to sit for a while, taking off my shoes to dip and swirl my toes in the current below. Closing my eyes, I breathe deeply, absorbing some of summer's most gorgeous scents and sounds, and allowing myself to be lulled into some much-needed relaxation. My mind bobs and hovers like one of the bumblebees circling nearby, aimlessly landing here and there and there and here until finally, slowly, alighting on the things that have brought me to this place, so very far from where I started. The things I've been running away from. Suddenly, yet in slow motion, my gossamer blinders slip away. *The bridal veil falls.* The truths (and lies) that my life has been built upon begin to gush outward, pushing past my tightly squinched eyes in a deluge of tears. The waterfall and I become one.

The crash of water cascading over the cliff's edge is good cover for the unexpected escape of my pain. My sobs. I've come here simply to immerse myself in the peace of nature's beauty, taking a break from searching the neighborhoods of North Carolina's

Blue Ridge Mountains for a place to start my new life. But sitting here in this beautiful place, in a state where I know no one, I'm overcome by my aloneness—not just today's, but for all my tomorrows and my past several years, too. I'm overcome by the crumbling pit in my heart, soul, and life that comes with facing the compounding loss of *till death do us part* and *happily ever after*.

Twenty-six years ago, I married the man of my dreams. Josh thinks I'm kidding when I say I fell in love at first sight, but it's true. Both of us were attending the same college in Kansas—Josh was a pre-vet student from Hawaii, and I hailed from Minnesota, studying to be an elementary school teacher. The odds of our paths ever crossing were about zero until the day we landed in neighboring dorms in this far-flung state. When our eyes first met across dining hall tables and cheeseburgers—when I felt the heat of our very first spark—I owed destiny the courtesy of paying it some attention. So I got myself a part-time job at the same place where Josh had a part-time job, and within a few years we were engaged. Fun, genuine, and easy to talk to, Josh was the nicest man I had ever met—and I was the luckiest gal in the world for half of my life.

College-degree-earning potential aside, during our early years as Mr. and Mrs., we didn't have much more than shared dreams and each other to cling to. But that's all we needed for taking on life's next great adventure—whatever that might be. One year became five years, then ten, fifteen, and twenty. New jobs, new states, and new countries; new kids(!), dogs, houses, and schools. Everything that evolved was somehow, wonderfully, both expected and unexpected at the same time—everything was unfolding just as it should be. Best friends and trusted partners, two halves of the whole—we were a team, forever. A devoted husband and dad, Josh was a great provider for me and our two sons. Funny, smart, and caring, he made it easy for us to roll with the punches and skate through the rare rough patches relatively unscathed.

Until the rough patches became minefields, and every which way we turned, something blew up.

As I sit here on my rocky perch, the splash of the waterfall and the buzzing of the bees fade away as I remember the memories. I see nothing, hear nothing, beyond the reels playing in my mind.

•

"I do."

Finally, the part I've been waiting for: *I do, he does, and the kiss.* I wasn't sure the priest was actually going to complete the ceremony after Josh and I lost our composure when the altar boy sneezed. For the last fifteen minutes, our shoulders have jiggled with silent giggles as we tried not to make eye contact or noise. We're both twenty-four, yet behaving like two little kids . . . the giddiness of love and happiness, I guess. Several months ago, we took the required weekend-long Catholic marriage prep course and were not at all surprised that there weren't any surprises—we talk about everything. And now it's official: I get to spend the rest of my life with my best friend.

Our wedding reception is held nearby at my parents' house— the place I've called home since kindergarten. A yellow two-story clapboard with black shutters, it's the perfect place to celebrate with family and friends. As Josh and I arrive, newlyweds, arm in arm, strolling up the sidewalk on this sultry summer eve toward the music and laughter, I feel the warm strength of my roots—this home, these people, this neighborhood that all had a part in raising me. Not too long ago, I brought Josh here to meet my folks for the first time, whispering to my mom that he was *perfect.* Now he returns as part of the family, and today we begin planting good, strong roots of our own.

I'm wearing the bridal veil Mom wore when she married Dad—a crown of seed pearls and layers of wispy lace—the once-in-a-lifetime symbol of tying the knot. (I might have worn her gown, too, if I could have gotten it zipped.) The bridesmaids are wrapped in rose-colored satin, and Josh and his groomsmen wear tuxedos and shiny shoes. We've never been so fancy. Happily posing for the photographer, we preserve every moment on film—cutting the three-tiered cake, tossing my bouquet of red roses, flinging the blue garter that my aunt wore to her own wedding, and chatting with my grandma, my dad's mom, my one living grandparent. A few waiters drift silently through the house, serving champagne and hors d'oeuvres, as a harpist plucks notes from the polished wooden harp my dad made with his own two hands.

Our day is a beautiful melding of memories, the promise of things everlasting, and dreams for our future.

And then, in a blink, just a few years after our big day, our family of two becomes a family of four, first with Joey, then Ricky, expanding our hearts and lives, and my full-time job becomes *Mom*. Oh, the joy and wonder of so many *firsts*. The first smiles and words, the first teetering steps, the first full-night's sleep. And the mixed blessing of that first morning when cartoons are a bigger draw for the boys than piling into our bed like squirming puppies, all arms and feet and elbows and butts.

Joey is three years old when we make our first move, from Florida to Minnesota, and Ricky is a newborn, swaddled in his soon-to-be-favorite blankie. Winter starts on Halloween, with a deep dumping of snow, and seemingly lasts until summer. So when the chance comes for us to move somewhere (anywhere) warmer, we do. And we keep on moving every few years to new states and new countries. I had sort of assumed our little family would be like the one I grew up in, staying in one place forever. But Josh's long string of promotions keeps taking us on new adventures, opening doors and unlocking experiences I could never have imagined.

We are living the dream—not just the vague dream I'd had of us all being happy and healthy together—but one that is all of that *and* even better.

Grade school and middle school, Houston, Spain, Louisville, and El Paso. Then, when Joey is entering tenth grade and Rick the eighth, Josh's job takes us to New Delhi, India, our most exotic move yet. A place of great adventure for our family, it is also the place where things for Joey start falling apart. Not exactly sure what is going on, when Joey graduates from high school, Josh and I agree it is wise to move back to the United States so we can be closer to our college-bound son than we'd be if we stayed on the other side of the world.

A short time later, during Rick's first week as a sophomore at his new high school in Maryland—and Josh's first week at his new job—Joey attempts suicide while drunk during his first week of college in California. Josh and I fly out to be with Joey, ultimately bringing our oldest child and all his squashed dreams home, just a week after we'd been out there helping to get his dreams all set up.

Three years later, Rick is graduating from high school, and my folks and Josh's sister are here to celebrate. But Joey is in jail. Again. Just a few miles away. Although we haven't talked about it, I can tell we're all committed to keeping *happiness* slapped on our faces for the entire weekend, bright smiles beaming through the dark cloud. Most of the benchmarks over the past several years have been horrible, so Rick's accomplishment, this occasion, is a real gift. And he needs to feel it.

It's been three years of arrests, court dates, overdoses and injuries, addiction treatment, and big fat lies and fights and fears. I've been consumed with saving Joey from the drugs that consume him, as well as saving my son from himself. I've been stalking my son, trying to out-manipulate his manipulations, and working to get him into rehab and to make rehab stick. It's been a full-time job trying to keep Joey alive, which hasn't left a lot of room in my life or head for anyone else. I feel like a terrible mom for whatever I did to have caused this and for not being able to fix this, and for abandoning Rick time and again when he also needed me most.

Josh and I still stand side by side in a crisis, even if we don't always see eye-to-eye day-to-day. Rarely do we agree on how Joey is doing, so Josh doesn't like to talk about it, and he spends more and more time at the gym. He's also taken up jogging and biking . . . basically spending most of his free time getting fit. I don't blame him. I talk nonstop about every lie, every action, every missing link; obsessing over Joey is my last remaining connection to him, and I can't let go.

In just a couple of months, Rick will be heading off to college—just a few miles down the road in Washington, DC—and life will be back to the way it was in the beginning: just the two of us, Josh and me, best friends, taking on the next new adventure. Except it doesn't feel like that's going to be true. We need to do something to survive all the gloom hanging over our soon-to-be-empty nest. Josh and I talk about doing more things together, like taking cooking or dancing classes, and how we can make our unexpectedly long-term temporary living situation more tolerable.

Still waiting to build our dream house, we're living in the tiny, old place we purchased as a "knockdown," so things like entertaining friends, planting gardens, and getting our furnishings out of storage have been hanging in limbo until Josh's promised promotion becomes a reality. We hire an architect to get the dream started on paper, at least, and Josh suggests building a patio in the backyard as an immediate, if temporary, fix. Instead, we decide to turn Rick's bedroom into a big walk-in closet, booting him out, even before he moves out, into his own walk-out "suite" in the basement. No longer do we need to climb behind chairs and rummage through puny closets all over the house in order to get dressed, which has, some days, felt like an enormous hurdle to me.

Josh's job has always involved a lot of travel, and I really never minded; since the early days, the boys and I managed to carry on and keep busy. But with Rick soon gone, the prospect of Josh's future travel looks different. It looks *lonely.* For the three years we've lived in Maryland, Rick and I have filled the after-school and homework hours together, with him teaching me how to play the card game Magic: The Gathering, or me teaching him to drive, or eating dinner while watching Jack Bauer survive the next hours in *24.* We're both kind of homebodies, which is comfy and safe. It's been a time of grounding and connecting in what has become a rocky world. But there will soon be a lot of empty hours bouncing around in this house, instead.

I've been careful in making new friends since moving here, not wanting to add the judgment of strangers on top of the shame, guilt, and blame about Joey and his addiction that I'm already carrying. But I'm in a different place now—I know the truth of this disease, so I'm done with living in shame and silence. I'm done hiding my story. I'm ready to step out and be real. The truth will help me to find more of the right kind of friends. What anyone else thinks no longer matters.

●

This first year of being alone together again—with Rick away at college and Joey, I don't know where—hasn't whisked Josh and me back to the days when our love started.

Last night I dreamed I was trying to get an egg from a carton. The first one I picked up had a crack, and so did the next one and the next. One was stuck to the bottom, so that when I tugged on it, it broke apart in my hand. One after another after another, some version of the same. It seems to me that my subconscious self was telling me that everything in my life is broken.

But, actually, my conscious self already knows that.

Joey has walked away from rehab. Again. Down in Florida. From the place I convinced the judge up here in Maryland to send him a few months ago. He thinks addiction treatment is a scam and says he will never go back. Spiraling out of control, in a familiar old pattern, he's been spewing anger and hatred between brief bouts of sweetness and love. The Addict and The Child, competing for the win. When Josh and I attend our most recent family program, I am a different mom than I'd been all the times before. I now understand that I cannot change or fix Joey, just *me*. But still, I try. And Joey is all I can think about. I live and breathe the fear that my son is going to die. So I'm dying inside as I wait for the inevitable to happen.

Josh has been shutting down—and gradually shutting me out—more and more since the nightmare with Joey's addiction began, but since Rick has been away, living his life as a college freshman, it's been worse. We recently had a session with a marriage counselor to help sort that out, but Josh felt like we'd joined forces against him and he won't go back. So, we're stuck. *I'm* stuck. I'm so *alone*. I don't know how to fix this. I don't know what to do or say. Josh won't talk about his feelings, or anything else, and he always seems irritated—his normally easygoing personality now has a biting edge. He keeps his headphones on or turns the radio up loud when we're together in the car, and he turns on the TV or walks out of the room when I'm talking, even if it's just silly chit-chat, not about anything that seems like it might make him sad or mad. He works late, eats out, and forgets to call. This isn't the man I married, and this isn't the man, the partner, I've known ever since. It seems like *this* man doesn't even like me. It seems like he is hurting me intentionally in the hope that I might just go away.

I'm just trying to survive this. Putting on a phony front. Trying to be something more than dead while I am alive.

The other day, someone asked me if having an addicted child is hard on a marriage—well, *hard* doesn't begin to describe it. Addiction is a devastating disease, and it destroys everyone it touches. I can see why so many marriages—and families—don't survive.

•

This afternoon, Josh returned home from the gym with a jaunty bounce to his step, saying how much he loved his life, seemingly unaware that he was hours late for a much-needed, hopefully healing date. And seemingly unaware that life as we now know it is not something anyone could love. This was just. Too. Much. Rick was here with his new girlfriend, downstairs watching TV, so I cornered Josh in our newly created walk-in closet, whisper-yelling that I deserve better than this, that I won't take crumbs, and that if he doesn't get a grip on his stupid midlife crisis soon, we might end up divorced. To which he replied, "Yeah, I guess I've been running away. I'll think about what I want to do." *I didn't really mean it! I was just throwing out the D-word to wake him, shake him up.* But there was a lot of unexpected answer in his quick reply.

I told Josh he has until August to figure out whatever needs figuring out, or he can leave. I added that, although the past years have been tough, *really tough*—with all the hopelessness and helplessness, the terror, shame, and guilt—I had meant it all those years ago when I'd agreed to "for better or worse, till death do you part," vowing to hang in there through whatever unimaginable hell life might throw our way. Even this. And I hoped he meant it, too.

Turning, I walked out of the closet, calling Rick and his girlfriend for dinner, and I served up a load of fake happiness along with the platter of meat and potatoes.

Now, it's the middle of the night. I cannot sleep. My heart and mind and soul are shredded. I'm sitting outside so no one inside will hear as I implode. Supposedly God doesn't give a person more than they can handle, but tonight I'm pretty sure that is false. I want to hold my family together, but I can't. I can't just let it fall apart, but *I* am falling apart. My family is the only thing that really matters to me, and yet it seems like everything I have done, everything I've touched, has broken. I did my best, and my best sucks.

Josh and I have been married for half our lives. That has to mean something. Heading back inside, I write Josh a note, set it on his nightstand to find in the morning, and crawl back into bed. I reach out to touch him, putting my hand on his arm, hoping that my love for him will sink in while he is sleeping.

> *Josh,*
>
> *I don't know how to say this without starting a fight,*
>   *or starting to cry.*
> *So I'm writing you this.*
> *I don't want our marriage to die.*
> *When we got married it was for better or for worse.*
> *And this has definitely been the worst.*

We have lost our son, our dreams, our hope.

*We've lost the things we used to do together, the little things
we did that made us a couple and a family.*

They are all gone.

*And we have built this wall, which has gotten bigger as we've
lost more dreams and more hope and more of the things
we used to do together, the little things we did that made
us a couple and a family.*

I have been so depressed.

But I have stayed.

*And if you had gotten sick and needed to be taken care of,
which would have choked off more dreams and more hope
and more of the things we used to do together, the things
we did that made us a couple and a family,
I would have stayed then, too.*

Because as hopeless as it feels, there is love.

*And if there is love there still has to be a little hope that we
can rekindle our dreams and the things that we used to
do together, the things we did that made us a couple and
a family.*

I will not beg you to stay.

But I want you to stay.

I love you.

Me

Josh doesn't mention my note, but I think I hear him crying in the shower the next morning.

A few weeks later, as I'm in the closet changing into my PJs for the night, he moves in for a hug—not a hug for me, a hug for *him*—and I recoil. I'm not feeling very comforting since I'm in such dire need of comforting myself. Josh says he hasn't decided what he wants to do yet, is waiting for something to "hit him." I can't help but think that the *something to hit him* should be me. He says he's been wondering what life is all about, what all the effort is for, adding he doesn't mean to hurt me. To which I reply, "Then don't."

Now, I'm in Utah, renting an off-season ski condo for three weeks in July, the weeks leading up to Josh's make-a-decision-on-what-to-do-with-us deadline, to focus on writing *The Joey Song*, a book to help other moms with addicted children feel less alone, while absorbing the serenity of the mountains. But this afternoon, sitting out on the deck, my feet propped up on the hewn-log railing, I'm writing in my journal instead. I started keeping a journal a few years ago as a way to find perspective and sanity within the vortex that is Joey's addiction, but it's been doing double duty for quite a while as I've tried to survive Josh's midlife crisis, too. And right now, what I'm writing makes me feel sick.

Josh joined me here for the first few days—which now seems like forever ago. We hiked the mountains for hours, we sat by the pool, we ate and drank and laughed—we had the best time we've had together in a long time. I was sure we'd made it over some invisible hump. As a lark, we looked at some of the condos for sale, imagining how nice it would be to have our own place when we come every winter to ski, knowing, of course, that's impossible for so many reasons—including the on-hold promotion and rebuild of our Maryland house, and the big elephant in the middle of our lives: *us*. But Josh has been talking to a bank about mortgage rates since he returned home, which makes me think that the midlife crisis is still in full swing. And after he encouraged me to stay here for a few more weeks, things started getting weird—and he sort of disappeared.

I know the wife is always the last to know, but I *know* Josh isn't having an affair. I know this with every fiber of my being, and yet I've learned a few things about denial and blinders and wishful thinking while dealing with Joey's addiction over the years. So I also know not to ignore all the flashing neon signs around me—and I haven't. Our marriage was built on a foundation of trust . . . and I've trusted. Now, however, for the first time ever, I'm suspicious.

Being here, I've become aware that Josh hasn't said *I love you* to me in ages—this became obvious at the end of our phone calls. The silence. When those sweet words didn't get repeated back.

Tomorrow I'm heading home—to what, I don't know.

●

If not for a receipt lying on the passenger seat of Josh's car, I don't know how much longer my torture would have lasted—how much longer Josh would have allowed it to last. But there it is, a strip of white paper, a receipt, sitting right where I am going to sit, once Josh has pulled his car from the garage and I go to hop in.

It was just last night that I returned from Utah, and now we're heading out to a movie and dinner, a *welcome home* date, but in the space of mere seconds, bits and pieces of the past meet the present, and the future is changed. I can see that the receipt is for cell phone minutes—something Josh's phone doesn't need—so I make a show of tossing it over the headrest and into the backseat, but really, it's crumpled up in my hand. Like a laser, my mind zeros in on a moment that barely registered when it actually occurred some months ago (or maybe even a year)—the time I heard something buzzing in our newly conjoined closet, which turned out to be a phone in Josh's gym bag. Laughingly, I took it to him, saying, *look what I found in your shoe!* And he laughingly said that in the hubbub of the gym locker room, someone's phone must have somehow fallen in. Now, I'm horrified at my naiveté. How could I have been so stupid?

After ordering popcorn and drinks, Josh heads to the theater and I head to the restroom for a closer look at the receipt. I'm trying to think up a logical explanation besides the one I'm already thinking. When I take my seat next to Josh, my heart is both sinking and pounding. The action happening on the big screen doesn't register; I'm looking inward, planning what I'm going to say to Josh once the movie is over.

We walk to a nearby restaurant and are seated outside on the bustling cobblestone promenade at the heart of downtown Bethesda. As soon as we've placed our drink orders, I burst, asking if he's having an affair. (Because of course, he is. It's so obvious.) He replies, "I'm so glad you brought that up. I've been trying to find a way to tell you this: I'm gay."

I just sit there, my mouth open to say something, something, something, but nothing comes out. Finally, I sputter, "If you think by saying *that* you're going to get off easier, you're wrong, so just tell the truth." Josh is smiling. No, *beaming*. (Free at last.) "Really. I'm gay." His relief, his happiness, is palpable. I, on the other hand, dissolve into a blubbering mess. *This is real. Josh and me, our family. We are broken.*

Once I've cried myself out (as subtly as possible, in public) and gotten some answers, I tell Josh that the most important thing now is for us to preserve the family we made, no matter what. Already shattered by Joey's addiction, we cannot allow this to be the blow that causes our family to completely fall apart. The boys are just becoming men—they need this from us; they deserve this from us. They need to know, to see, that love can last forever. As parents, we must keep doing our job.

I will need some time before telling Rick and Joey this news—I think it will be easier for them if they don't see me so fragile. Josh and I agree to work on building a new normal, a foundation of strength, just the two of us—a new kind of best-friend-ship—before he moves onward with his new life. By the time Rick is home for Christmas break, we should be pretty solid in our new relationship. We'll get Joey up here and have a few weeks to process this seismic shift in our world, all together.

Josh doesn't want me to tell anyone his news yet—not my friends, not my parents, not anyone. He wants to share the news himself when he's ready. I guess I understand that, since I need some time before telling our own children. But I already know that keeping this huge secret is going to be lonely.

·

Today, I'm fifty. A fifty-year-old phony, pulling a fast one over on my adult kids. Just one month after Josh's announcement, we're celebrating my birthday as a way to get the whole family in one place—I want us all to share one last nice memory together, just in case. Josh and I don't know how the boys will take his news or if, once it's out there, there will be any *family* left—there's only so much a family can take.

Josh, Rick, and I have come to Florida, trying to make it easier for Joey to join us since his presence at family events has been sporadic for years. Sitting at the head of the table, surrounded by the three loves of my life, I'm aware of how picture perfect this celebration must look to anyone watching—and how that image couldn't be further from the truth. There's nothing about my day, my life, that is as it should be. It's a sham. Nothing is as it seems. The waiter brings out a fifty-candled cake, everyone sings, I wipe my eyes, blaming my tears on the smoky little flames. My heart aches for Joey and Rick—they have no idea of the pending occasion we'll be bringing them together for next.

Josh is a cork, zinging through the air in jubilant celebration. His true self has been shackled for so long that he is, understandably, rejoicing in this new freedom. I think he feels safe and loved and relieved, and so he is back to being his old, nice self. But I feel alone in carrying his secret and really need some support and love and hugs.   .

Rationally, I understand why Josh wasn't able to embrace his truth back in the 1980s, why he pushed it down and married me instead. It would've been unimaginably difficult for a young man to enter adulthood burdened by the stigma so pervasive at that time. He would've been sentenced to a life of judgment and scorn from all corners. I get that. But, my life, *my* truth, was built on his truth—which wasn't even true—however justifiable the denials and lies. If Josh could have been honest with himself, I would have married some unknown someone else, someone for whom I wasn't simply *the only other option*. A space filler. I would be secure in the love of someone to grow old with, having strung together a lifetime of years, the meaning of which would not now be in doubt.

The rug has been pulled out from under my life. Everything that was and is and might yet be has been sent flying. Consciously or unconsciously, Josh has known for his whole life what I have known for only one month. It's going to take a while for me to collect myself and find a safe place to land.

I've been wondering why it was so hard for Josh to tell me his truth once it began to seep out. Once he realized he could no longer contain it. *Why, why, why?* He should have known the conversation would go pretty much as it did, which was nowhere near as difficult as the prolonged hell we've been living for years. *Why?* He should have known what my reaction would be. We'd already talked about sexual identity back when we were talking through all the possibilities, the inner turmoils, that might have been driving Joey to use alcohol and drugs, so Josh should have been secure in knowing this would never affect my love. Why didn't he trust me to stand by him as he worked this out?

We've been going on long evening strolls, holding hands, talking things through, and figuring things out. I think we can do this. I think we can show our boys, the world, how to do this transition thing right.

•

Rick calls to tell me about a big Halloween party next week, and he's wondering if I'd like to take him out for lunch and costume shopping. He's a sophomore this year, and I'm glad his college is close enough for us to do stuff like this. Especially now; I want to sneak in as many happy times with him as possible before what's coming comes. Rick already knows he wants to dress up as Sasquatch or a yeti or something else big and furry, but he's in no rush, so we spend a few hours roaming the aisles of a sprawling Halloween store as he entertains me with his commentary and poses while trying things on.

He's never said anything, but I'm sure Rick has noticed the changes in his dad's behavior—and mine—over the past few years and is sort of assuming that the adults in charge will somehow get things back to right. We've started jogging, Rick and I—an activity we can do with his dad—weekend runs, 5K races. He probably thinks this means we're all happy again now (instead of surreptitiously building a new foundation for him to stand on once he comes to understand that the foundation he's been standing on all along is seriously cracked). My heart pinches with sadness at what I know is blind trust.

I've been thinking about moving once Josh and I finally separate. Somewhere near the mountains. Maybe Asheville, North Carolina. Financially it makes sense, since we'll have two homes, and the DC area is so expensive. But mostly, then I wouldn't have to be the person people feel sorry for around here. On the other hand, if I stayed here, Josh and I would be able to establish a closer relationship. *And Rick.* I don't know if I can leave Rick. I need him in my life. And if he needs me, I don't want to be too far away, too soon.

Last night I had a dream that Rick and I were walking in the neighborhood when we came upon a group of men working on a big hole in the middle of the street. They were trying to support the sides with wooden beams in order to keep the hole from caving in, but as we watched, the ground began to crack and crumble, radiating outward. Rick and I turned and started to run toward home, looking over our shoulders to see if we were running fast enough to stay ahead of the earth trying to gobble us up. I woke myself up when I hollered out, "Rick, save yourself!"

•

Pointy shards of glass are exploding outward from the center of my universe. I'm trying to catch them and keep them safe. Or put them back together into something whole. Or just *something.* Anything.

A moment ago, I was standing in the kitchen, talking with Josh. Now I'm crumpled on the coir rug where our dog sits when we wipe his muddy feet after coming in from the backyard. Grabbing myself in a fierce hug, my hands are like claws, digging into the skin on my arms, drawing blood. Anything to out-pain the pain

I feel in my soul. I'm howling. Josh sits just out of sight, around the corner in the living room. Waiting, I suppose, for me to regain my composure and sanity.

It could've worked. It should've worked. Our agreement to work on building a new kind of best-friend-ship before he moves onward with his new life. But Josh couldn't do it. He says he didn't understand how our arrangement was supposed to work.

The bridal veil falls.

Josh still wants to keep everything a secret, but I can no longer cope on my own. I've been avoiding talking to the people who love me, feeling like a liar by living the lie I've been subjected to living. My isolation cannot go on. The hurt and confusion and loss have been unbearable. I call my mom and dad, a few friends. *And the boys.* We make arrangements for them to come home over the Halloween weekend, months before originally intended, for our first-ever pre-planned and serious Family Meeting. I'm still fragile. I'm *freshly* fragile. Again. I don't know how this will go.

•

Today is the day I've been dreading for months (following a lifetime of believing this day is a day that would never, ever happen). The end of our family as we've known it.

The brake lights on Josh's car flicker as he reaches the end of the driveway. He's on his way to pick up Joey from the airport—Joey hasn't been home since his one night of freedom between jail and court-ordered rehab shortly after Rick's high school graduation, well over a year ago. I wait about an hour, nervously pacing the house, before leaving to pick up Rick. He is waiting in front of his dorm when I drive up, tense and ashen. He doesn't say a word when he gets in the car. And neither do I—it's not possible for me to speak; I can barely breathe. But a few choking sounds escape as I try to swallow some wadded-up tears.

We arrive back at the house just as Josh's car pulls in, too, and Joey greets me with a silent hug. Although I'd kept it pretty vague when arranging for the boys to come home, they know they're here to talk about something important, and they know no one is sick. It's clear from their demeanors that they know whatever we're going to talk about isn't going to be anything good.

In preparation for this day, I've been talking to a therapist. She said it's important for Joey and Rick to know that Josh wondered about his sexuality back when he was in his teens so they won't be wondering if a surprise discovery might strike when they're in their late forties—adding that it's critical that Josh be the one who tells them. Josh said he was hoping to just tell them we are getting separated and leave it at that, but I said, "No. They need to know the truth. No more secrets and lies; our family needs to be done with that. The boys need to know that being gay is nothing to be ashamed of—and they need to know that *you* believe being gay is nothing to be ashamed of. We don't know if either of them might be hiding this secret, too. And Joey needs to know he didn't cause this; addiction destroys a lot of marriages, but ours isn't one of them. If you don't tell them all the truths, I will."

Now, plodding into the dining room, we pull out the chairs surrounding the dinged and scratched old round oak table. I hold on tight to the edge of my seat. And Josh speaks.

"So . . . I'm gay. I suspected I was gay when I was in high school but set it aside until fairly recently. Now, I've decided I need to explore this. For several months, your mom and I have been working through this. There's lots of sadness, but no animosity; we're hanging on to our history of love. We are now going to be a *nontraditional* family, but we'll always be a family.

"We're going to do a legal separation instead of getting a divorce, and I will continue to take care of your mom financially; she'll never have to worry about that. Mom thinks she wants to move to North Carolina, so that might happen within the next several months. It's beautiful and centrally located to everyone, but she'll stay with me for all future visits; nothing will change for us as a family at the holidays and special occasions. Your mom and I still *love* each other, but we are no longer *in love* with each other. We have twenty-five years of friendship, but in order to maintain that friendship, we need to live apart.

"The saddest part of all this is the hurt done to you boys. Your mom and I will always be here to talk, and we'll always be open and honest. We promise. Mom is seeing a therapist to help sort through this, and each of you might want to talk to a professional, too. Holding stuff in isn't healthy. Talk about this with whoever you need to.

"Just as I hope you won't let this change in our family define you, I hope you won't let this define me, either. But do let this define your mom; even though this has rocked her world, she has been supportive and compassionate, and she has kept you boys and the family as our main focus."

Stunned relief. That's what I see on Joey's and Rick's faces. I can finally breathe. And speak. Josh and I answer their questions—we talk and talk and talk. And then, all of a sudden, the doom cloud lifts. Rick leans back in his chair and jokes, "Well, Dad, what did you expect, running around in all that spandex?" And Joey, pushing back the hair flopped over his forehead, smiles, and says, "Whew, I'd thought I was in trouble. This is nothing!" That's it. For now, this is no big deal. Somehow, miraculously, we—all of us—did good.

I do wonder, though, how things would have unfolded if Josh's and my roles had been reversed. How would Josh have reacted to me from the beginning of all this? And how would he and the boys be reacting to me now?

●

I call Rick to see how his Halloween party went—and to check in on how he's doing. I want to see if he's okay now that yesterday's news has had a little time to sink in. He says he didn't go to the party after all, that it no longer sounded like fun. I think about how excited he had been when we were shopping for his costume, so happy, so unsuspecting, so carefree—and how Josh and I then went and squeezed the air out of life, out of family, as he knows it. Of course, Rick is hurting, no matter how strong and supportive he acted yesterday. It pricks at my heart, imagining the shaggy Sasquatch costume all wadded up in a ball in a corner, a sad pile of reality and deflated dreams.

Rick says he's not bothered at all that his dad is gay; there are so many gay people on campus, it's just not a big thing. He says he and Joey had talked on the phone before our Family Meeting, and all they could guess—because all they could do was guess—was that Josh must have been having an affair and we were getting divorced. So it was a relief for him to learn that his dad hadn't betrayed me in that way. A relief to learn there is no reason for him to be mad. But he says he feels sorry for me—he says I'm the one who drew the short end of the stick.

Last night, after we had talked everything out, everyone went their separate ways to decompress or celebrate or cry or whatever. Joey has not yet reemerged or responded, so I don't know how things are looking or feeling to him today.

●

Josh has lost his job. Just weeks after our Family Meeting, and after a decades-long career climbing up the corporate ladder, for the first time ever, he has fallen off. And it hurts. I don't know how to bandage all of our family wounds.

A friend of mine said, "Well, things could be worse; at least you don't have to deal with something like surviving the earthquake crisis in Haiti." I've heard this sort of thing before, about Joey and his addiction: "At least he doesn't have cancer." I understand that people unintentionally say insensitive stuff when trying to be comforting, but dismissive comments like these hurt. Sure, things could be worse, but no one has walked in my shoes, my days, my heart, my life. Suffering isn't a competition.

With everything on hold until Josh finds a new job, we continue to stay together in our never-to-be-rebuilt old house on the hill for a couple of months, trying to work on building a new *us*. But an uncorked cork (Josh), and whatever you call a thing suspended in midair after being flung afar by a violent shake of a rug (me), cannot coexist under the same roof and remain friends. Or sane.

So tonight, we part ways.

Together, over the past few days, we found Josh a tiny furnished apartment and packed up his things, and today we got him all moved in—sock drawer organized, shirts hung in order of color, family photos on a shelf. Now, before I drive away into the night, before leaving Josh in his new place to start his new life, he gives me a little something to hang on to: Josh tells me that he realizes he wasn't very nice to me for a few years; he hadn't meant to be that way, and he's sorry. We hug. We cry. Although the love we knew is finished, it doesn't just end.

I've just said goodbye to half a lifetime together—the lifetime that was but wasn't really. And to half a lifetime more—the lifetime that was yet to be.

When I return home, the house is so silent. So empty.

Oh my God. I am now *just me*.

•

It's Valentine's Day. A few months after moving out, Josh has invited me to lunch at a local restaurant to celebrate our newfangled kind of love. As I slide into the booth, he says it was difficult to find just the right card for this day. Well, he couldn't have found anything more perfect than the card he handed me, which says, "You Are My Very Greatest Earthly Blessing." I have goosebumps. Maybe that will be the title of my next book. A story of a love that is stronger than the cracks in its foundation and bigger than the boundaries of marriage. *A blessing bubble.*

Now, over pasta salad and wine, Josh is saying he's ready to start dating.

Bubble popped.

Of course, I knew this would be coming, eventually. But still, I'm not prepared. I don't want this. I don't want Josh sitting across the table from someone who is not me, giving that someone a card full of love like the one I just received—only more romantic. And I don't want to know all of his personal milestones going forward. We've been trying so hard to be friends, buddies, pals, even though we're still married. Our boundaries are blurry. And confusing. And painful. (For me.)

Josh says he is transitioning. "Well, actually," I say, "you've been transitioning for years. Now I need to do something to move forward with *my* life." I ask Josh to move back into our house-that-is-not-a-home when his lease runs out so I can get a small apartment of my own, keeping me sane until he has a new job and I can make my permanent move to Asheville. The house we moved into as a family four years ago is not a home. It is a prison. The life we set out to build there, and everyone who was in it, is gone and changed. For too long, I've been sitting on a nest of shriveled dreams and wishes, trying to keep something warm that I know doesn't exist. I need to take a step outside of the nowhere I've been trapped.

Until these last few months, I've never lived alone. Josh and I were married right out of college, so I've never known the insecurity of setting out on my own. But I can no longer be a placeholder in someone else's life.

·

Bridal Veil Falls. I'm back in the here and now.

The sun's slow slide across the North Carolina sky has gone unnoticed by me until this moment, as it dips behind the waterfall's edge, casting a shadow across my foot, my knee, my thigh, gradually pulling me back to the present, to where I sit, perched on my rock, hearing again the sounds of the cascading water and buzzing of bees.

Shuffling through the layers of memories and varnished truths that brought me to this place has taken its toll; I'm emotionally exhausted.

Gathering my things, I stuff my towel and sunscreen into my backpack, then tie my sneakers into a sloppy sideways bow. I stand, sighing, rubbing the indentation that still encircles my finger where my wedding ring used to be, and take one long, last look at Bridal Veil Falls before turning to leave. I have another week of house hunting ahead of me before returning to my apartment in Maryland. I've been taking steps toward leaving the pain hovering over my life behind me. But I've got a long path ahead.

2

When Truth Wears a Veil

I am homesick for a place I am not sure even exists.
One where my heart is full. My body loved.
And my soul understood.

—MELISSA COX

EARLY THIS MORNING, long before dawn, it vaguely occurred to me—as I lay flat on my back on the kitchen floor, eating strawberries—that stress upon stress upon stress, apparently,
can't be contained with a pasted-on smile.

Sometime around two in the morning, I woke up to go to the
bathroom but took a quick detour to the kitchen when, suddenly,
I felt funny. Light-headed. Like maybe I needed a glass of water.
In my tiny apartment, the trip is only a few short steps, twelve
at most, but before I could reach the sink, my inner world went
black. Felled like a log, I slammed to the floor. Sometime before
dawn, I regained consciousness, facedown on the hardwood in a
pool of blood—my forehead, nose, and teeth feeling crushed. And
then, sometime within the next hour or two, I was able to roll over
onto my back, battling the wild storm that whirled and twirled
my brain and eyes with the most minuscule motion of my head.
Sometime later, parched, weak, and wonky, I made my way to the
refrigerator, scooting along at a speed of about two feet an hour,
while lying flat on my back, trying very hard to keep my head still.

Prying the refrigerator door open from the bottom, I felt around for something, anything, to give me the strength needed to make the trip back to my bed. To my phone. To call a friend for help.

I'd been sort of hoping to come across a bottle of water, but still, I was relieved to find a crackly plastic pint of unwashed strawberries on which I could slowly munch and quench my thirst. A rubbery cheese stick or a floret of raw broccoli wouldn't have been the same.

Sometime after sunrise, I made it to the side of my bed, nudging the carton of strawberries alongside me—the carpet in the bedroom making the last leg of the difficult scooting-journey even more so. Looking up from my position on the floor, my now-mountainous bed seemed insurmountable. Even though that was where my cell phone lay, cozily tangled up among the covers, my brain and eyes still swirled wildly at the slightest movement of my head. A concussion, I was pretty sure. But I wasn't at all sure I would ever move beyond where I lay, on my bedroom floor, again. But sometime around noon, I somehow hurled myself to a successful landing on top of the mattress. Sometime soon, a friend arrived, followed soon after by an ambulance.

And sometime, during or after all that, I decided that being alone is scary and that moving to Asheville, where I know no one, is no longer an option.

I think I've known this truth since my house-hunting trip a few months ago but have been in denial. I think I've been trying to make things fit even when they didn't, because I wanted to fit somewhere that isn't *here*. Somewhere without heartache and wishes clinging to every corner. The *flight* part of *fight or flight*, I suppose.

Several friends, and even Josh, joined me at different times while I was in Asheville, supporting me as I tried on life in the Blue Ridge Mountains for a month. It was so fun. An adventure. Until, toward the end of my stay, during the space of a few days when I was alone, my usually well-behaved inner-me went rogue. I was strolling around downtown, looking at local handcrafted wares in shop windows, when suddenly my legs became heavy and I couldn't breathe. I felt pain in my chest. And terror. I did *not* want to have a heart attack in the middle of the sidewalk, but I couldn't make it to where my car was parked a couple of blocks away, so I sat on a nearby bench, hoping and praying this thing would end one way or another without me having to endure a big scene.

After a few more such episodes and a few phone calls, I understood that my "heart attacks" were actually panic attacks, and the fear of having another panic attack seemed to cause another panic attack, which made me afraid of having another panic attack . . . a debilitating cycle that continued even after I returned home to my apartment in Maryland. For a few weeks, I was paralyzed by this fear of fear. I tried to outsmart my inner self, but in the end I needed the help of an SSRI, a nonaddictive antianxiety medication. The beast that reared its ugly head was not going to rule my life, my *new* life, just as I was trying to shape it.

Now, back at my apartment, the plastic band from the hospital still encircling my wrist, I'm gingerly nursing the injury to my body and brain. In a fog, I shuffle to the bathroom for a look in the mirror, trying to assess the damage done to my face by my middle-of-the-night faint. All swollen and bruised and blood-streaked. I'm a mess. I realize that I've been living in fear of something happening to me while I'm alone—something that would lead to a lingering and sad, long overlooked death—since the moment Josh's words changed my life last year. And my body and brain have been busy trying to make my fears come true. It seems my subconscious has been screaming at me to understand that running away—to a place where I'd start off completely alone—is a mistake.

I'm not ready to leave Rick. Or my friends. And support. *What was I thinking?*

My little apartment is cute and within walking distance of restaurants, movie theaters, and walking trails, and hopefully Rick will come to think of it as home base. Hopefully, *home is where the mom is*. And whenever Rick needs either, I will be here. *Here*. In Maryland. Where I belong. I can move forward without moving. Without moving what remains of our little family apart.

•

After Josh asked me to marry him, nearly thirty years ago, we soon took a trip to Hawaii so I could meet his family and see the place where he'd grown up. I had never traveled anywhere that involved flying over an ocean, or to a place that had palm trees and rain forests and beaches not-on-a-lake. So, for an entire week, I was agog. I got to see where Josh graduated from high school, the veterinary clinic where he had worked, and the stable where he'd ridden his horse around barrels. And I got to hear funny stories about my betrothed, like how, when the family was all packed in the car and heading down the road, Josh would do double takes at horses as the car zipped on by, when all of his brothers were doing double takes at girls. We shared some good laughs.

But now I realize, during that one particular funny-storytelling moment, Josh's perspective would have been more informed and completely different from mine. And everything we had that came before and came next was built upon a layer I didn't even know existed.

Did Josh ever really love me? I don't know.

The truth has been wearing a veil since the day we met.

All along, I had believed we were soulmates, and I had believed that Josh believed that, too. I had believed that the trust, the intimacy, the momentously personal moments we shared, were deeply felt, by both of us, and real. And I had believed that the evolution of things—things like muffin tops and wrinkles—went by nearly unnoticed, softened by the rosy hue of true love's colored glasses. But now I believe I shouldn't have believed any of that. Now, I wonder about everything, because nothing was or is real. I wonder, since I was merely filling the role as Josh's only socially acceptable option in life, did he see me as a duty he must endure? A noose? From the beginning, his perspective and reality have been different from mine. How long, really, have I been alone in this marriage? How long has the meaning and feeling behind our vows been a solo show?

Why was Josh so angry with me over the last several years? So unkind? Was I the embodiment of whatever it was that was holding him back? Of whatever was keeping him from being who he was meant to be? Was he resentful of me, our marriage, my presence? Why didn't he just tell me about this thing I didn't know?

Even though I understand *why* Josh needed to conform to the norms of the time—find a nice wife, make a family, not be gay—it doesn't change the fact that he built *his* life on *my* life on top of an enormous lie. His need to pretend to be someone he wasn't took away my chance to be with someone who was real.

I'm left wondering if half a lifetime of memories full of happiness and love might not have been what they seemed, either.

I remember our first year together as newlyweds. Josh is finishing his last year of college, I'm teaching first grade at a nearby Catholic school, and we take on the hobby of breeding lovebirds, a messy and noisy hobby for a two-room apartment. Our diet is heavy on ramen noodles, Velveeta, and hot dogs because that's what we can afford—and that's the type of cuisine I know how to cook. I remember the first time I set our little fake-wood table with some of the china and crystal we received as gifts from our wedding, pulling it out of the cupboards for our first Thanksgiving, just the two of us—turkey on a platter, bowls full of trimmings, goblets and cloth napkins—feeling all posh and grown-up.

I remember Joey's pirate-themed birthday party when he is five. The boys "help" Josh and me to build a big pirate ship in the backyard—we wrap black landscape fabric around long wooden stakes pounded into the grass, making sure the ship will be spacious enough to hold the small swarm of pirates soon to arrive. We paint portholes on the hull and a skull and crossbones on the sail before hoisting the mast. After we draw a treasure map full of landmarks and helpful dashes (then crumple it up and burn the edges with the flame from a candle), Josh and I set out to hide clues around the neighborhood, dig a hole for the treasure chest, and lay down a big red cardboard X to mark the spot.

I remember Rick's fifth birthday party, too. Josh and I sneak away to bury a few hundred plastic-yet-prehistoric dinosaur bones in the sandy expanse of a nearby playground, creating an excavating adventure for the little paleontologists who will be helping to celebrate Rick's big day. We choose a place right in the middle of this archaeological dig to build a towering volcano, scooping sand and filling the center with a mix of ingredients ready to erupt in a froth of red lava at just the right time.

I remember the quiet excitement of Christmas Eve, little Ricky still believing in Santa, and Joey still pretending to believe. The tree lights are twinkling and the candles are flickering as we sit around the dining-room table to enjoy our traditional meal of Cornish game hen. Rick is more inquisitive about what he's eating this year than last. "Is this the butt? A bird butt—an itty-bitty bird butt. I'm not eating something with a *butt*. Butts poop." (Sigh.) After we tuck the boys into bed, after we're sure they're sound asleep, Josh and I sneak around, collect presents from the closets and corners where they've been hiding and place them under the tree. I put the cookies and milk and carrots on the kitchen table; Josh sips and nibbles and gnaws, and then sprinkles around some crumbs.

I remember the Beanie Baby craze. (Oh my.) McDonald's has just added Teenie Beanies to the Happy Meals, so Josh and I pile the boys into the car and we spend half a day driving around placing orders and eating fries until we've collected every single one of the mini must-have cuties. Times two.

I remember eating dinner together, the four of us, every night—unless Josh is traveling, and then we are three. I remember Joey and Rick helping Josh and me as we rake leaves, and pick peaches, and crank out some ice cream, and clean the garage. And I remember the closeness that comes with moving every couple of years, the comfortable and familiar rhythm of packing boxes and embracing our next great adventure.

Are the love and happiness of my memories real? Or was Josh pretending this, too? Was he resigned to plodding his way through an unfulfilled life? Was our time spent together an eternal sentence of *going through the motions*?

I remember our move to Spain, carried in on the winds of Josh's latest promotion. When we arrive, the boys and I don't speak any Spanish, but Josh is fluent, thank goodness. He is our voice and translator until we learn enough to get by on our own. Rick is in preschool with a dozen other kiddos from a bunch of different countries, speaking a bunch of different languages—French, German, Thai, Spanish, and English—and yet somehow they've been able to communicate from day one. And now, as Rick yells out a warning to his little buddies that a grilled cheese sandwich is "hotta, hotta!" he is totally understood. Joey is in first grade, and while most of the kids in his class speak at least some

English, he is learning Spanish in much the same way as Rick—casually, among friends.

Our first Thanksgiving arrives just a few weeks after we do, and I need to do it up just as if we were at home—I don't want the boys to miss out on all the traditions. But, since my Spanish reading-and-speaking vocabulary consists of very few words (and none of those words happen to be words for the foods we plan to eat for the upcoming feast), pulling together the ingredients from the local shops is a challenge.

Most important, of course, is the turkey. But there are no Butterballs all nicely cleaned, wrapped, and labeled at the end of the meat aisle of the grocery store. In fact, there is no meat aisle at the tiny grocery store in the nearby town. I need to go down the street to the butcher shop for that. So in I go. The butcher shop is small, and the meat display is the only thing to see upon entering; all the meat looks very much like the animal it came from and I am not used to that (and some of the things I'm looking at are looking back at me). There are no whole turkeys behind the glass case, so I inquire about this. Well, actually, I say, *gobble, gobble, gobble?* hoping the kind-looking silver-haired butcher behind the counter will understand. And I mime with a quick slice of my neck with my finger for *off with its head,* adding slicing sound effects for good measure. And then I do the same on my arm for *off with its feet,* followed by dramatic performances of plucking the feathers and pulling out the guts.

Later, over dinner, I tell Josh and the boys I'm fairly confident that I ordered, and will be picking up, a plucked, gutted, headless, and footless turkey in seven days (seven fingers). But I feel like the whole turkey-buying experience was unnecessarily gruesome.

Exactly one week later, I return to the butcher shop, Rick in tow. He's three, so he is eyeball-to-bulging-eyeball with the shiny, red, skinless goat head in the glass case. Fearing nightmares, I cover his eyes with my hand. The butcher remembers me, I can tell. Disappearing into the back for a moment, he returns, beaming, arm raised high, holding an enormous pimply pink turkey upside down by its feet, like a prize. The head is gone, but I can see this bird is still full to the brim with its innards, and while most of the feathers have been removed, there's a long way to go. Well, we have a turkey. We'll make it work—I don't have the words, or the heart, to try making any corrections anyway.

The next morning, there's excitement in the air. Joey and Rick are bouncing around in the kitchen, eager to help stuff the turkey and get it popped in the oven. Josh, assessing the task ahead as too traumatic for their young eyes, says, "You two, out!" Closing the door behind them, Josh and I attempt to tackle the turkey. Well, actually, Josh does most of the plucking and pulling and rummaging around inside the bird. Mostly, I'm just making noises that reflect the expressions playing out on his face. Eventually, tuckered out from the tussle, Josh says that even if he's able to get things under control, after what he's been through already, he's not going to be able to eat any turkey for dinner. *My thoughts exactly.* Feeling guilty but beaten, we throw a perfectly good but unconquerable turkey into the trash and take the boys out for pizza at the Italian restaurant down the street, managed by a Chinese family, in Spain. All those efforts at making Thanksgiving as traditional as possible, and *traditional* it isn't. But, surprisingly (to me), it turns out just fine anyway.

A few days later, one of the moms waiting at the school asks me how our Thanksgiving went. It's easy to read her shock at our sheer ineptitude and waste. She grew up in a home where chickens ran around in the yard, and it was nothing to grab one by the neck and give it a brisk twirl or quick lop, and hang it upside down on the back porch to drain. Before moving here to Spain, I felt like I knew pretty much everything about everything, but I already realize I actually know pretty much nothing.

Thanksgiving is a holiday best shared with a crowd. As are most holidays, I think. So the next year (and the next and the next) we gather the friends-like-family we've made here, sit with them around our table, and give thanks. Plates are piled high with turkey, cranberries, and stuffing as we share our newly tweaked old tradition, just as our friends have shared the traditions of their home countries—and their hearts and homes—too.

Our four years in Spain are magical as we learn, grow, and bloom together. Or maybe not. I don't know anymore if the magic of my memories—the magic I had thought Josh and I shared—is real.

•

India is a busy place. There's a lot going on everywhere, all the time. Although Josh and I try to keep our home as much like *home* as possible, a haven where the boys can retreat from the constant chaos and noise, India still seeps into every nook and cranny. It cannot be contained. Every glimpse, every inhale, brings something new for all of us. Every moment is a new experience—and either an adventure or an ordeal. India can be overwhelming and exhausting, frustrating, heartbreaking, and infuriating. But it is also the most richly textured and colorful place imaginable. I love it.

Rick is thirteen when Josh's job takes us to New Delhi. Joey turns sixteen just a few weeks later, so we fly off to the Maldives to celebrate his birthday for a week, scuba diving and swimming in the Indian Ocean, making a big deal of his big day since he hasn't been here long enough yet to have made any friends. This trip is also meant to give the boys (and Josh and me) a brief break to absorb some of the initial shock from the place we've just moved to. Because *shocking*, India is.

We live in a three-story house across the street from the American embassy and just down the block from the embassy school, where Rick is in eighth grade and Joey is in eleventh. A guard is always posted at the end of our driveway to let people in and out through the black iron gate. He sits in a little white pointy-roofed hut, often snoozing. It's a fairly relaxed situation, unlike our next-door neighbor's small battalion of machine-gun-toting guards who hunker down behind a small sandbag-stacked fortress. On top of our roof, there is a huge round vat that stores water so we don't have to wait in long lines, carrying buckets, during the sporadic times when water, for most of the permanent residents of New Delhi, is supposed to be available. Our neighborhood's red-bottomed monkeys have figured out how to open the vat's enormous lid and have been going for long, soaking swims, so the lid is now padlocked. We have different, purified, water delivered for drinking, cooking, and washing fruits and vegetables so we don't become violently ill. But sometimes we still do.

It takes me a while to notice that I've never seen a garbage truck here, and to figure out how the household garbage process works. Whatever we toss into our wastebaskets, the housekeeper collects and takes to the kitchen, where the cook adds it to the food-prep waste and sets it outside the back door for the sweeper, who puts it in a cart and hauls it across the street. But first, our trash is picked through by everyone along the chain—the housekeeper, the cook, and the sweeper, followed by the gardener, the guard, and maybe the driver—for whatever might be considered worth keeping. Whatever remains is what the sweeper wheels over to the towering and stinking pile of garbage on the sidewalk outside the embassy walls. Here, barefoot men, women, and children crawl around searching for whatever they can use or eat or sell, and hairy hogs and rats and flies and rot, I guess, eventually take care of the rest.

Since cows are considered sacred here, we don't eat any beef. We just drive around the emaciated bovines as they roam the streets, plastic bags often dangling from their teeth. Our meals have consisted of chicken, chicken, and more chicken, until last night, when the cook cooked up some steaks. Usually, I guide the cook in planning our meals, making sure the boys get to eat familiar foods here at home, but sometimes he'll whip up a repeat of a past success or surprise us with something new he thinks we will like. Like last night's steak. It was a bit tough, but it was a meal with no chicken, so *yay!* This morning, while in the car with the driver, I told him about our unusual dinner, asking about our cook's mysterious connections . . . and he told me that yesterday morning a car had hit a cow in front of the house, and the guard had run to tell the cook, who had run out to chop off a hunk of meat, along with the other interested cooks in the neighborhood. Standard operating procedure. When I share this bit of information with Josh and the boys at dinner tonight (chicken), Rick says, "Great. We ate roadkill." Poke, poke. "What's this? Roadkill raven?"

Our family is acutely aware of the sheltered and charmed life we've lived—and continue to live. The poverty, the hunger, the suffering are everywhere. And it's heart-wrenching. But we're finding ways to make a difference while we're here. No kindness is too small. Joey brought home a street dog and her pups, and Lucky now lives on our large covered porch, safe, comfy, well loved, and well fed. (She's skittish about coming inside—has never known *inside.*) And I've been bringing home babies, five to be exact, from the orphanage where I volunteer. They live with us, one by one, sometimes for months at a time, with the whole family helping to provide the tender loving care these babies need both before and after life-altering and/or life-saving surgeries. Surgeries that end with all five babies being adopted to loving homes. For Joey's Eagle Scout project, he recruits the expat community and local marines to help build, haul, and install an expansive playground structure for orphaned children who've somehow never before climbed a fort, slid down a slide, or swung on a swing.

There's a lot going on here behind the scenes. There are layers upon layers upon layers of mystery. But it's not only India that isn't all as it seems.

In the hubbub of acclimating to our chaotic, exotic new world, Joey is changing. Josh and I think we're dealing with teenage, not troubled, behavior, until our sweet boy turns shockingly mean, volatile, and thin, and living in denial is no longer possible. Over the phone, in consultation with doctors in the United States, Joey is tentatively diagnosed with an eating disorder, which seems both logical and extremely ironic, considering where we live. Leaving Rick in a foreign country with new family-like friends, Josh and I take a now-even-more-unhappy Joey to a clinic in California for treatment. Josh returns to Rick shortly, but I stay with Joey on the other side of the world, far away from my youngest son for four months.

When we return to India, Joey finally seems happy, healthy, and back to his old self. Whew. A single renegade thread tucked back into place. He graduates from high school with several college scholarships to choose from, and Josh takes a new job so we can move back to the United States—we want Joey to have his family and home in the same country as he is. But Joey is arrested on his way to college, tries to kill himself once he gets there, and, it turns out, his eating disorder isn't actually an eating disorder at all, but addiction.

Not only had Josh and I been putting together the pieces to the puzzle wrong. We had been putting together pieces to the *wrong puzzle.*

A skill, I now know, at which I'm quite adept.

•

Recently, Josh told me that the acceptance he's gotten from the boys and me has been tremendously helpful in enabling him to figure out his real self. That warms my heart. Here we are, separated, and Josh has definitely moved on, yet we're still attached by caring. This certainly doesn't match the sparkle of what had been my dreams and wishes, but Josh is in my friend pile, and I'm in his. Which is so much better than being in the discard pile. Or no pile at all.

> *Sandy,*
>
> *I've been wondering how to recognize a wedding anniversary in our situation. Our marriage is the best thing that ever happened to me—I know I am a better person for having you in my life and being married to you—but I know that I have hurt you and have pulled the rug out from your life and what was supposed to be. So maybe the best thing I can say is that, as I look back over these twenty-six years, I am so very grateful for you, and I hope the joy that we experienced is not overshadowed. And to use your words, I will be eternally grateful for what we have become during this past year versus what we might have become.*
>
> *I love you.*
> *Josh*

All of this love and kindness is, well, lovely, but it's such a head-achingly confounding switch from the past several years. What does *this* mean? And what did *that* mean? I'm trying to figure it all out. And some other things, too. Like, why did Josh lead the architect and me to believe we were all working on creating a dream house for so long (instead of, in actuality, dabbling in delusion)? And why did he try to buy the impossible ski condo in Utah—and to build a frivolously temporary patio on our knockdown of a house—just months before sharing his long-overdue news? Why did he need a secret phone? And why was it easier for him to push me away in hurtful ways than to be (still hurtful but) honest? It's pretty clear to me now that Josh had one foot out the door of our life since we moved from India to Maryland. It's pretty clear that we've had no future for years.

Was it the pain of his child's addiction and the death of his dad, his last living parent—two crushing events happening at the same time—that broke the walls of his decades-long self-containment? Was Josh so full of suffering from living with me and his secret that the only way for him to survive these new pains in his heart and soul was to set his old pent-up pain free?

It's not healthy for me to look backward. It won't change anything, other than possibly unearthing things that might make a friendship with Josh impossible. So I need to focus on *now*. As with Joey's addiction, I need to look at the big picture—I need to focus on the goal and not sabotage it. With Joey, that means *not helping The Addict to kill The Child I'm trying to save*. And with Josh, my goal is for us to *remain a family*—so I need to focus on making a devastating situation less so. Even if that means putting on some very selective blinders.

Also, as with Joey's addiction, I think we should shine the light on this thing. I think we should talk about the truth of what has broken up our marriage and family, not keep it a secret, not lie, not hide it as though we're ashamed. My human opinion (not necessarily my ever-changing, shocked-to-the-core-wife opinion) is that Josh is a good man—a kind, smart, spontaneous, funny gentleman—who also happens to be gay. So what? But Josh still wants to keep it kind of hush-hush, fearing, I'm sure, getting crushed by harsh and hurtful remarks just as he's emerging like a butterfly from a chrysalis into his new life. Experience has probably already given him good reason for wanting to seek safety in the shadows. But we have the power to change the stigma around this thing that should carry no stigma. By being honest and open, we have the power to help others feel free to be whom they are meant to be—feel free to love and marry whom they want. Which, eventually, will put an end to the unintended consequences, the collateral damage, that *not* marrying whom one wants inflicts on families such as ours.

Not everyone is comfortable with things they don't—or won't try to—understand. And so they judge; it's much easier to make a snap judgment than it is to pause for a moment and try to see things from a different angle. To slip on some unfamiliar shoes and imagine how things might look and feel when walking someone else's road. But it's a precarious place to be, up on a high and mighty pedestal. All superior. And perfect. And right. I know, because having a child with the disease of addiction swiftly and roughly knocked me off my place on that lofty perch. Things, all things, look much different when living them up close. So, I *now* know that the only person I should ever judge is myself, with an eye toward personal betterment. *That,* not passing critical judgment on others, is what will make a difference that matters (and isn't "for the greater good" the ostensible reason for being all judgy?). Leaving the world a better place than on the day I arrived is, I believe, my ultimate purpose here on earth. So I'll leave the judging of others up to the only judge who matters.

•

Rarely does anyone ask about Joey anymore. I don't think they know what to say. They don't want to make me sad, that's very clear. But they also don't have the words for this horrifying thing that continues to unravel, and unravel me, year after year.

I don't know how Joey feels now, many months after the bombshell news about his dad and his family. After it's had some time to sink in. I don't know if he's okay, or if it rocked his world, or if whatever is happening up here doesn't even matter since he's far away—and has been far away in so many ways—for so many years. A few days after our Family Meeting, Joey returned to Florida, and true to his word, after he walked out of treatment a few years ago, he never went back. But a picture emerges through retreating girlfriends, or landlords looking for rent money, or police who find a backpack full of his life possessions abandoned on the beach, that life is not easy for Joey. His struggle continues. Not long ago, I sent him this message, which, hopefully, he at least carries in his heart and mind:

Dear Joey,

I miss you. I ache for you to fill your place in my life.
Will I ever again feel your hug? Hear your laugh? See you
*   proud?*
I don't want you to be an addict. I don't want you to push
*   me away. I don't want you to die. I want you to be sober*
*   and happy and to fulfill your dreams and fill your soul.*
*   I want you to be Joey. But addiction is sucking the life out*
*   of you. Sucking the you out of you.*
I'm haunted by the difficult life you are living; I'm sad for
*   the life you could have but are missing; and I grieve*
*   for the loss of my son who is still alive.*
I made a lot of mistakes trying to help you, sometimes treat-
*   ing you like an adult when you were acting like a child,*

and treating you like a child though you're an adult.

I tried warm fuzzy love and I tried tough love. I tried keeping you from hitting bottom, bringing the bottom up to you, and getting you into treatment when I thought you'd hit bottom. And I struggled to recognize the difference between helping and enabling—I tried so hard to stay on the right side of an invisible line between helping you to live and helping you to die.

Through trial and error and lack of results, I learned that I can't fix this for you. And I learned that I love you enough to bear the toughest love of all.

Sometimes love means doing nothing rather than doing something.

But, Joey, Letting Go is not the same thing as giving up.

There is a place in my life that is exactly your size.

I'm keeping it warm.

Love,

Mom

I wish my love were enough to fix Joey's addiction. But if that were possible, his addiction wouldn't have stood a chance. Sadly, only Joey can fix this—or Joey will die. I cannot *love him* better. (Or love him *better.*) All I can do is *love him as he gets himself better.* This is a hard truth to accept. But accept it, I must.

For too many years, I thought I was helping Joey. I thought I was doing my job by keeping him out of trouble and getting him out of trouble and believing his lies. I snooped and stalked and tried to out-manipulate his manipulations. I did everything and anything to make things right. I tried to keep my child from suffering, because that's what a mother's love does.

I loaned Joey money when times were tough, but not wanting to make times any tougher, I didn't ask him to pay the money back. I made excuses for Joey's new self-centered meanness, and I pretended not to hurt when he missed my birthday or when his place at our Thanksgiving table remained empty. I believed Joey's explanations for his sunken eyes and shaking hands, and I believed his convoluted denials of drug overdoses and emergency room DOA revivals. (Well, sort of.) When Joey was arrested— the times I knew about—I showed up in court as a reminder that he was loved and had reason to head in another direction; I even stayed when he bared his teeth at me and hissed. I wrote letters to the judge (damage control) pleading for Joey to be sentenced to rehab, not jail. And then I listened as Joey blamed everyone he could think of for why he did end up in jail; the only person not to be blamed was the one looking at me from the other side of the smudgy glass.

Three times Joey was convinced or cornered into going into addiction treatment. And three times Joey played it and everyone around him like a game and then walked away. I connived. I wheedled. I cried. I begged. And I continued to aid and abet and enable like a champ.

I did everything I could to protect Joey from himself until finally I realized it wasn't him that I was protecting. I was protecting The Addict. Making it easy for The Addict. Giving The Addict one more day to further consume *my son's* body and mind. And life.

So, my motherly love needed to be contorted and redefined.

There's nothing about fighting my fierce maternal instincts that is easy. But I'm not doing what needs doing for me. I'm doing what needs doing for *my son*.

Every April, I fly down to Florida, hoping to show Joey that I'm full of love and open arms—*even if my hands are tied*. Hoping to show him that my love is constant. In case he ever wants to come back. I don't ask questions about drug or alcohol use. About things over which I have no control. Instead, we enjoy the moment, eating burgers, talking about things that aren't likely to veer into precarious territory, laughing, and making happy new memories to hang on to. For both of us. When it's time to go, I hold him tight, wrapping him in my arms, feeling the power of our dusty bond. A silent exchange of hope and strength and eternalness, of a love that has been bruised but never broken. I kiss his cheek, leaving a lipsticky mom mark, and then, again, I let him go. I open my arms—empty but now full—which will keep him snug and close to my heart until next time. Next year. In letting go of Joey, I'm holding on tightly to so much. In letting go of him, I'm letting him know that I believe in him. That I believe he will, someday, find his way back.

Until that day arrives (hopefully)—until Joey returns healthy and happy and whole—I need to do something with the pain clawing at my heart and soul. I need to do something with my maternal need to *do something*. So, in conjunction with my women's group and a local group home, I start Bistro Boyz, a program teaching twenty at-risk teen boys how to cook and grocery-shop on a budget, so they'll feel comfortable and confident with all of this when they move out on their own.

Every week, a different team, made up of Bistro Boyz and a few volunteers (Bistro Galz), takes a trip to the grocery store to shop for the ingredients on their list—everything needed for the meal they, as a team, planned the week before. Beef stew, apple pie, au gratin potatoes, green beans, whatever seemed yummy to the Boyz at the time. And the next night, they prepare their meal together in a small dorm kitchen, trying out new skills, new foods, and new gadgets, before enjoying the meal they've cooked, seated around the long table—passing food and sharing stories and laughs—like a family. The cycle of four teams repeats each month.

A week before Thanksgiving, the whole bunch of us—all the Galz and all the Boyz—cooks up a traditional feast with several turkeys and all the trimmings to share with the group home staff and the entire women's group. It's quite a crowd. We use the facility's professional kitchen for this big job, with the head cook showing us where things are to be found (and where things are to be returned), good-naturedly accepting the rowdy invasion of his space. We set up a conference room for the holiday buffet with long tables and white tablecloths. And the Boyz, wearing aprons and chef hats, proudly serve up their culinary creations to the dozens of enthusiastic guests before loading their plates and sitting down to join them. Someone stands to give thanks for the good food and great cooks. And silently, so do I—cooking with these young men is helping me to survive.

I don't know much about the lives of the teens that we cook with. Only that they're in the group home because of difficult circumstances. And that's all that matters. For whatever reason, the mothers of these young men aren't able to do mom stuff for them right now. But I am. And maybe someday someone will do some mom stuff for Joey.

•

Turducken. That's what I'm cooking up for Thanksgiving this year. A turkey stuffed with a duck stuffed with a hen stuffed with herbed stuffing. The breast bones have been removed to make the stuffing of bird-inside-bird possible, so while it's big and beautiful, it's flat on top instead of rounded. It's *different*, but that's the point. I'm shaking things up. A few weeks ago, while talking about the upcoming holidays, someone asked me if I wished things could go back to the way they were before. Well . . . yes. Yes, I do. But they won't. They can't. And dwelling on that or trying to re-create that—the *before*—is where pain lives. And so I'm try-ing to avoid all of that. I'm trying to make a new tradition for us, something Rick will still find tasty and fun. And happy. Our holi-days have already been shrinking for a few years, with Joey's chair at the table remaining empty or his stocking hanging on the man-tel untouched. Yes, holidays have been hurting for a while. But I can take control of the holiday instead of the holiday taking con-trol of me. Even if Josh is off doing whatever he's doing. And Joey is wherever he is. Maybe homeless. And hungry.

The other day, on the hunt for some fall decorations to spruce up my apartment for our little Thanksgiving Day feast, I went to the garden center where Rick worked during high school, and where he still works whenever he needs a little extra money and over college breaks. He wasn't there, but one of his coworkers rec-ognized me as Rick's mom. She told me what a nice young man he is, someone to be really proud of, and that, as a mom herself, she knows we don't always hear the good stuff—and Rick is *good stuff*. It felt so good to hear this. Because as the mom of an ad-dicted child, I often feel like a failure—even though I know addic-tion is a disease and that parental imperfections cannot cause it. So, as irrational as it may be, it is a huge relief to know Rick is turning out okay, and that I didn't somehow ruin him, too. Note to self: scatter kindness—a warm word or two can completely change someone's day.

A few weeks ago, I lost Rick's baby blanket—his *blankie*—the blankie I've kept tucked away in a safe place for over twenty years. The one piece of his childhood still remaining after all our moves. The well-worn, well-loved blankie he dragged alongside him or wore wrapped around his neck everywhere he went when he was little. It's gone, and I'll never get it back. I'm pretty sure it didn't mean anything to Rick anymore. But it meant something to me.

And it means something that I lost it. Well, I *left* it. I left it behind when we finally sold our house, where Josh had been living until we did.

The house we were going to knock down and rebuild is now in the realm of someone else's dreams. But before that could happen, we needed to get rid of all the things that none of us needed or wanted or had room for, which was pretty much everything remaining. This year, Rick moved from the dorm to an apartment where the décor is *four college guys*—well, he's only let me in once, before any of his roommates moved in, saying ever since, "No, you wouldn't like it," so I'm only assuming. And my apartment is too small to accommodate one more thing. So Rick and I went over together before the estate sale that Josh arranged began, more for one last look at *life as we knew it* than one last look for *stuff.* It wasn't until the sale was over, after the house on the hill was sitting dark and empty, stripped of every last remnant of its most recent occupants, that I realized I'd left behind Rick's blankie, the only thing that had really mattered.

As we strolled through our forsaken collection of belongings, Rick and I were silent. Seeing the hand-scrawled price tags stuck onto the things of our life for the soon-to-begin scavenger hunt was hard.

The antique cabinet made of mahogany and wavy glass where we stored the things we had used for special occasions. Most of the special-occasion things we kept stored in there, too. The paintings on the walls. The fondue pots the four of us would sit around on New Year's Eve, dipping cheese and meat and chocolate, talking and laughing until beginning the countdown to ring in the next best new year together. The bread maker that would fill the house with warm and tasty aromas on autumn weekend mornings. The frames for the family photos (of a family that no longer exists).

The entire master bedroom—the bed, the nightstands, the dresser, and lamps. Our family history, marked for sale at 90 percent off.

As we left, driving down the steep driveway for the very last time, away from the house we'd moved into after returning from India five years before, I looked over at Rick, trying to assess how he was coping with this latest aftershock. Before I could ask, he said, "Well, that was weird," and went on to share his observations on things, like how he'd forgotten about his dad's old record albums until he saw them again, how crowded the rooms seemed with everything out on display, and how ridiculous it was that someone had put a price tag on our old broom. Rick is always free with sharing his *thoughts* with me, but not his *feelings*. So I can only guess about those.

A year after losing his job, Josh remains unemployed, a real shock considering his long, stable, illustrious career. I'm afraid he's been too busy uncorking his new lifestyle to focus on what he really needs to be focusing on. And I feel resentful that the breakup of our marriage seems to be like a no-longer-bottled-up bottle of bubbly for him, while I'm left dangling midair over the rug that he pulled out from under my life.

I spent four long years waiting until Josh finally told me what I needed to know in order to make sense of the life that was falling apart around me. And now, I've spent one long year more waiting, again. Waiting for him to do what he needs to do so I can piece together some of the crumbs and create a new life for myself. So I can move forward from this limbo, a limbo that keeps changing. A limbo with no clear end.

This waiting is killing me. My future feels very much out of my control, and I'm becoming afraid. I can't sleep—ever since moving out on my own, I have trouble falling asleep and staying asleep and getting back to sleep. Worry and aloneness, I think.

Even though Josh and I are living in two separate households, I manage all the bills, and what I see is an unsustainable mountain of expenses—some necessary, some not, and a lot of extravagance. Josh needs to get a job, soon, so we can get divorced and divide up our lives and our finances. I no longer want to pursue a legal separation as we had originally discussed—I need a division between us that is more clean-cut.

Josh has been the breadwinner of the family since Joey was born, almost twenty-five years ago, and I will always need to rely on him to fill that role. I stopped teaching to raise a family and to move us around the country and world every few years, which worked out perfectly for us. But now, as a woman over fifty who hasn't worked outside of the home since my twenties, I'm keenly aware of the precarious reality of my situation. Even though I'm very capable at many things, I've got nothing to show for the experience and talents I've accrued during my many years of married life. Nothing that matters in the working world, anyway. My résumé is blank. Out in the real world, I'm not worth more than minimum wage.

I don't know what lies ahead. What I will need to *accept*. What I will need to *handle*. What I will need to *figure out*. I feel powerless; I've *felt* powerless, like I'm being smothered under the hands of another, for years.

That truth wears no veil.

I keep pretending that I'm doing just dandy, but I'm not.

Where Love and Divorce Meet

Magic, beauty, strength & grace don't happen because
"shit was easy". They happen because we've courageously
dealt with whatever life served up & we gave ourselves
permission to transform the muck, both new & old, into
soulful, holyfire purpose. That's it. & Amen.

—TANYA MARKUL

NOTHING HURTS A MAMA'S HEART more than a child who's hurting. I know the agony of loving a child suffering with the disease of addiction—I know how it feels to live each day grieving the loss of a child who is still alive. And I know the anguish of abandoning one child while trying to save the other. I know real pain. So with Josh, as devastatingly painful as everything has been, the hurt is, relatively speaking, *nothing*.

The motherly battle against Joey's addiction has been one long, hard fight. A fight between hanging on and letting go, barely hanging on and hanging in there, surviving the unexpected, and just. Trying. To. Survive. And it has been a fight to protect my family from being utterly destroyed in the wake of addiction's toxic spread. I've made a lot of mistakes—and I'm deeply saddened and permanently scarred—but I'm also stronger and wiser. (And I'm gratefully surprised to find that I'm tougher than I knew; life before this had been very kind, so my toughness had gone untested.)

So I'm much better prepared to face what life hurls my way *now* than I would have been otherwise. I now know about controlling what I can, and self-care, and not making things worse. I've been learning, living, and breathing all of this while figuring out how to cope with Joey's addiction for many years. I have a well-worn basket full of tools to use in handling the disintegration of life as I knew it with Josh, and to handle it with some bit of grace. But, as always, *knowing* what to do is much easier than *doing* what needs doing. *Feelings* are to blame for this, I think—sneaking themselves in, between the *knowing* and the *doing.* Feelings are complicated, and sometimes the damn things make a mess of *doing the right thing right.*

Tonight, I cracked. I cracked like glass under pressure right in front of Rick, and I kept on cracking, even as I knew I should pull myself together so I wouldn't blow him and everything else that matters apart.

Rick has been living with me in my apartment, on and off, since graduating from college a few months ago. The job market for young folks fresh out of school is pretty dire with the economy having dipped into a recession, but Josh found Rick some sporadic temp work in New York City—where Josh now lives, and at the same Fortune 500 company where Josh has (finally!) found a job—and Rick stays with me between stints. I love having him back home, my newly minted adult child with his easy smile and charm. I love having the company, *his* company, and I love having someone to cook and eat and talk with during the times he is here. He's been learning to make pecan-crusted salmon for dinner and has introduced me to the miracles of a rice cooker, we've been seeing all the latest action movies, and when he had a job interview here, I was almost giddy with excitement at being able to take him downstairs to the apartment manager, who helped me to help him tie his tie. Tonight, we decide to walk out the service entrance and across the cobblestone promenade (aka, our back-yard) for a drink, stopping in at the very same restaurant where Josh pulled the foundation out from under my world three years ago. Just a stone's throw from where I now live.

I had thought I was stronger than the last time I was here, but it turns out I'm still pretty fragile right under the surface.

Until tonight, even as the years I've been kept on hold have dragged on (and on and on and on), I've kept a tight rein on my words about Josh and me and our still-nothing-happening divorce; I've not shared my feelings with Rick, except those on which I could put a positive spin. But for some reason, tonight, I crack. Before the waiter returns with our wine, the first tear is spilled. I think I'm as surprised as Rick is at the breach in my com-posure and what comes gushing forth. I tell him that waiting all these years for Josh to set me free has crushed my spirit, that I'm resentful of his dad dragging me like a tin can behind a shiny new car for so long, and that I feel like Josh has used me as a stepping stone, twice—once when we got married, and now, again, as he's been slurping up the security and comfort of my support while running off to launch his new life. I can see that my pain and my words are hurting Rick, but I don't stop, pausing for only one hic-cupy moment when the waiter returns with our drinks and some menus for snacks. I say that Josh has moved on so far and fast from his past (me) that I'm afraid I'll soon be nothing to him but a distant memory . . . then, just an inconvenient monthly pay-ment . . . and then, eventually, I'll be left in the dust, eating cat food, all alone. I say that I can no longer pretend everything is fine when everything has been, and still feels like, a fraud.

Rick doesn't know what to say, of course; this is his dad I'm talking about—and our relationship. I don't think any child, of any age, needs or wants to get an earful about parental strife; that's what friends and therapists are for. I *know* better than this. I can *do* better than this. I can *be* better than this. I begin to pull myself together. Slowly.

I don't say this to Rick, but festering underneath everything I *did* say is my belief that it's not only my life that was built on a lie. Joey's and Rick's lives were built on that lie, too. They spent their entire lives believing we were a happy family, unconsciously soaking that in as part of who they were, who they were just becoming, and who they were going to be. And now, everything they thought they knew and thought they had—the foundation on which they had grown up—is gone. My boys are now adults, but the destruction of a family hurts a child of any age. No matter how old they are, there are sure to be repercussions.

•

Today is the day I begin my new life. Three years and four months after my old life ended.

My lawyer sits next to me at the long conference table, shuffling papers around as I start to cry. A big, messy cry. I rummage through my bottomless purse for tissues. He looks uncomfortable, although I would think he'd be used to this part of the divorce process by now. He's around the same age as me; this is not his first rodeo. We've been in negotiations, with a mediator running between where I sit and where Josh sits with his lawyer in the room next door, since this morning. It's now midafternoon, and I'm feeling completely overwhelmed and vulnerable and discarded. Love and money—it all comes down to a show of how much Josh thinks I'm worth versus how much I think I'm worth (and how much we both think I might need to survive). He is laughing in the other room, a big belly-burst of amusement at something. I can hear it over my runaway sobs. When the day's ordeal is finally over, Josh and I run into each other out in the hallway, caught in the act of trying to depart this office building as quickly as possible. We're now face-to-face and red, puffy eye-to-eye, instead of the more safely anonymous room-to-room. He puts out his arms, tips his head to the side, and moves in for a hug, but I take a step back. The distance between us has grown much wider today. I'm not ready to embrace fake closeness.

In trying to be comforting, friends and family have used phrases like "At least he didn't leave you for another woman," not understanding how painful it is to have a husband leave by choice, no matter the reason. I've also heard several versions of "At least your husband didn't die. Imagine living with the loss of *that* love forever." Well, this divorce *is* a death for me. Losing life's love hurts deeply. The difference is that with *this* sort of death, the fond memories and feelings meant to carry us through such great loss are destroyed in the process. With this sort of death, grieving loses its protective softness.

I'm now an *ex-wife*. A subtitle I never, ever, imagined I would one day own. And Joey and Rick have parents who are now exes—so they now both have an *ex-family* and a whole *ex-life*.

More than anything, I hurt for my boys. Josh and I were supposed to make a life that would leave them secure and happy as they made their own lives—as parents, that was our whole job—not kneecap them just as they're stepping out the door. More than anything, I hurt that we, their most important examples, have shown them that love can't be trusted to last forever. I call Rick. He doesn't answer, so I send him a text message instead. *If you want to talk, I'll be home all day tomorrow. In case you need a place to put your feelings about what happened today.* I don't call Joey; I'm not sure if he, caught in the haze of addiction, knows about, cares about, or can cope with our divorce. He's never asked about the status of anything since our long-ago Family Meeting, so I've not mentioned it, either.

•

Sandra Swenson. I've changed my name back to the one I grew up with. Early on, I had intended to keep my married name, a glue that would continue to unite Joey, Rick, and me as a family, through eternity. Early on, that had seemed really important. But as the years have passed, I have realized I can't wear the name of someone who didn't want me. That's a burden I cannot bear, not even for my sons. But the truth is, it's our love and our history, not our last name, that bond us together. This is the glue that will hold us through everything.

I've moved again, this time into a historic old school building divided into condos. After the divorce a few months ago, it seemed wise to start making payments toward ownership of the place where I live instead of continuing to rent. It's located outside of my usual social and shopping path, but it's an affordable, recently renovated two-bedroom unit with friendly neighbors. It's *home*. All is good.

Rick was here for a week over Christmas with his girlfriend. We played games, exchanged gifts, had a gingerbread-house-making competition, and ate too much of everything. It was perfect—the only thing missing was Joey (and I was missing him *very* much).

This morning it's snowing outside, so it's a good day to stay home and start taking down the Christmas decorations. I've left them up a little longer than usual, hanging on to the holiday happiness that graced my new place, but it's time to put them away. Off with the ornaments, the tree topper, the lights; I'm making good progress. My cell phone rings, and I leap through a small mountain of crumpled tissue paper and shove aside a few boxes to find it. It's Josh, all excited to share some news. He is getting married—he proposed to his husband-to-be last night.

Well, that's something I didn't see coming.

(Again.)

I'm not crushed or hurt . . . or feeling anything, really. (Numb?) Just surprised. Very surprised. It's clear now that when Josh was divorcing me just over two months ago, he had a whole different, hidden perspective of reality than I had, just as he'd had a whole different, hidden perspective when he proposed to me long, long ago—back at the time of the first deceit, on top of which all further deceit was piled. So I guess I do feel something besides surprised. I'm also feeling deceived.

The Bistro Boyz program continues. I'm spearheading the creation of a cookbook full of favorite recipes from my women's club members—we need to raise funds to cover the cost of the groceries for our weekly meals with the young men. And I'm writing. Writing, writing, writing to finally finish *The Joey Song: A Mother's Story of Her Son's Addiction* and (hopefully) find a publisher. For a while, it was hard to focus on my book with so much else going on. But now, I'm back. There's healing to be found in putting words to paper. And I have something to say. I want to share my story to help change the way addiction is perceived and treated—helping to remove the shame, blame, and guilt harbored by other parents (but especially moms) on this same journey, and also within the community, and, therefore, within Joey himself. I want to help empower the moms who feel so powerless in the wake of this terrible disease, to help them see that even in their helplessness, there is actually very much they can control. I want to give moms the book I had wanted, *needed,* to read early on, showing that our love is not a failure even if our children have not yet found recovery, and that we can still find recovery of our own.

I have a mission. A purpose. A passion.

At his request, I send Joey a copy of *The Joey Song* manuscript via email. He reads it on his phone, on a bus, on the move from one side of Florida to the other. Joey replies, via text:

> *Your book's amazing im very impressed and im learning or realizing a lot I chose to either forget or pretended never happened . . . im not done yet but I'm going to get copies out if you seriously do want it published. . . . I know two people that can do it for you. Thank you so much for everything you have done for me, for every hug and word of encouragement, thank you for being my mom, I love you.*

•

Trying to settle my unsettled heart (I guess?), in less than two years, I move from my condo in Maryland to a house in the suburbs of Austin, Texas. My mom and dad said I should move back to Golden Valley, Minnesota, back to my roots, but I said, "As much as I'd like to be near you, it's way too cold up there, so *that* will never happen."

I keep saying I'm done moving, but this time I mean it. Really. I live across the street and down two houses from my dear friend Cindy and her family. We met while living in India and started the Moms' Circle of Love project together, which included working with the nuns at local orphanages, as well as with local doctors and hospitals, to provide surgeries for babies in their care who would otherwise, most likely, either not survive or remain unadopted. Cindy is also the person I trusted to take care of Rick when Josh and I left India, taking Joey to the hospital in the United States for medical help. So I'm now living (very, very) near friends who are like family, a connection I really needed. I walk over to Cindy's for coffee in the morning, or she'll walk over here for a glass of wine around five. Almost every day, at some point in time, we'll sit out on one of our patios or at one of our kitchen counters and talk and talk and talk.

Financially, this is a smart move. The cost of living in Texas is far lower than in my former neck of the woods, which was in close proximity to the very expensive Washington, DC. And I had really missed having an outdoor space of my own to imagine, create, and tame—it had been a long time since I could play around in the dirt. My garden here is already a beautiful oasis. In retrospect, the condo purchase was a result of my need to hastily plant a stake somewhere, anywhere, just to have a place, *my* place, after being left adrift for so long. But, also, it was another necessary baby step toward *coming into my own*. And once Rick settled into a full-time job in New York, I was ready to take my *next* baby step and move to Texas. (I never anticipated there would be so many *next steps*. I somehow thought I'd have both me and my life figured out quickly. Done and done.)

It was six months ago that I moved here, back in April, but I've been completely moved in since the end of month four. I'm a *do it and get it done (and done right)* kind of gal. Every box is long unpacked, every picture is hung, and vines of purple wisteria are hand-painted over the master bedroom windows to match the view of wisteria I planted to grow on the pergola outside. Just as with every place I've ever moved into (not counting the myriad temporary living places around all those moves)—a total of nine houses in three countries since being married, and three after that on my own—it's important that a house becomes a home as quickly as possible. Settled. Comfy. With a feeling of permanence (even though—and maybe because—the permanence didn't actually ever last). It's now September, and my new house has been *home* for months.

Josh got remarried last week. Before his wedding, I sent his husband-to-be an email, wishing them a wonderful life together. And I sent Josh a text saying *there's nothing I wish more than for the two of you to know love to its fullest, forever.* Josh had invited me to attend the big event—to be held outside at their newly built beach house in Delaware, atop their temporarily glass-covered swimming pool—but I just couldn't. As I told Rick, his dad's best man, "I wish them well on their big day, but I can't watch it happen." Contrary to the assumption of everybody who knows nothing about this, just because Josh married a man instead of another woman, it doesn't make the fact that he chose to marry someone else hurt any less.

As of today, *The Joey Song* is published. It's out there on bookshelves across the nation for people to (hopefully) buy. To hopefully find worthy of reading. But it has taken a whole lot of years to get to this celebratory point. Writing *The Joey Song* has been cathartic, but it's also been crushing at times, especially since the very sad and very real-life story has continued to be lived all along. I've had to set my writing aside, sometimes for extended periods, to collect myself (and new thoughts); sometimes, when sitting down to try making sense of all the troubles and feelings, it just hurt too much to try to go on. And then came the challenge of keeping what was happening between Josh and me separate from *The Joey Song*—the unexpected depth of and reason for our rift. The challenge of keeping the story focused on its intended message, without getting pulled in directions that would take it off track. But for the past five years or so, I've plugged away, and today, right now, I've just opened a box full of copies of *The Joey Song,* sent from my publisher. Today, I'm an *author.*

About a year ago, I created a website for parents of addicted children (particularly moms) and started writing a blog. And then, from the mysterious expanses of our great, interconnected world, came requests for me to speak at events for other people trying to wrap their heads and hearts around the addiction of loved ones. *Public speaking.* That was something I had never anticipated. Until the first invitation, I'd thought of myself as *a mom who is writing* and had never looked beyond that. I'd just been trying to throw my *writing* voice out there, hoping someone might want to *read* it. I'd never spoken publicly, ever, about anything—I even avoided taking speech class in college till my last semester, hoping they would change the curriculum requirements before I had to submit to the torture. I would never have guessed I'd have the confidence to speak in front of groups large and small. But purpose and love can change everything.

And so, as new doors are opening, I'm following new paths and seeing where they lead. Near and far, traveling by train and plane and automobile, I've been meeting with roomfuls of people just like me, parents who feel the same fears and pains and who have said and done and thought the same things. We know everything important there is to know about one another before the first word is spoken. To an untrained eye (and heart), we might appear to be a roomful of strangers, but we are already friends.

My new life, my new purpose, is starting to take shape.

•

Back when Josh and I were newlyweds, I didn't know how to do much of anything practical. I could barely balance a checkbook, I didn't know how to iron Josh's white cotton button-up shirts, and I wasn't a very good cook. I'd spent my whole life up till then, for the most part, just going to school and having fun (with, of course, some part-time jobs thrown in there to tie things together in a happy mix). But as I matured into the evolving roles of wife, working woman, mom, and *the one who stayed at home,* I discovered there was a very capable and organized person hidden away inside me, ready and willing to bloom. As time and Josh's career marched onward and upward, I began to manage everything having to do with running a home—budget, bills, minor household repairs—preparing me well for that aspect of living alone. Now, I'm not worried about being able to do what needs doing to run my new life smoothly. I can take care of myself.

Except when I *can't.* I'm still afraid of some version of the *I've fallen and can't get up* scenario happening, with no one knowing about it until it's too late.

During my first few years of living alone, before taking on a periodic, precarious project such as climbing a tall ladder to lean over a curving stairwell to change a lightbulb while standing on one leg, I would call one of my friends to say, "If I don't call back within five minutes, come see if I'm dead." But now, since my new house is a one-story with the HVAC headquartered in the attic, I need to climb up there to change the filter once a month. A precarious project, yes, but there's no more *periodic* about it. For a while, I would call my friend across the street, Cindy, with a heads-up before undertaking the dangerous feat—before pulling the long string on the little door in the hallway ceiling while ducking out of the way to escape being clonked on the head as the heavy wooden folded ladder came dropping down, and before climbing up on a separate, smaller ladder, to reach the side beam of the *attic* ladder so I could unfold the whole thing while avoiding being smashed in the face.

But sending out monthly pre-SOS signals isn't helping me to feel, and be, independent, and it's *not* helping me to *not* feel like a nuisance. So I find a new lightweight accordion-style, really nifty, and easy-to-manage metal ladder replacement—something I feel I can comfortably grow old with as I begin my fifty-fifth year.

When the handyman comes to install the new ladder, he brings a friend to help. As the three of us are talking about today's attic door project, he pulls on the string—and a big, fat rat falls out, hitting the floor with a thud, just missing landing on the handyman's head by an inch. It must have been sleeping right on the door. At first, none of us knows it's a rat. Or that it's alive. It could be a hunk of baloney sausage or a small sandbag falling from above for some reason. For a few seconds there, we're all just stunned. Until the rat finds its legs and starts to run. And as it runs into the guest room nearby, I run in the other direction, toward a kitchen stool.

The handymen are now rat catchers—well, one of them is. The other one is hollering out rat-catching tips from his place on the stool to my side. Feet off the ground. Just like me.

For the next twenty minutes, there's a lot of lunging and leaping and squealing going on, by everyone (and everything) under my roof, until, finally, the rat is caught and carried out to the street by its tail. As I watch through the front door window, the victor pauses a moment to pose for a selfie, holding the dangling rat high, then tosses it across the street. The rat bounds away, seemingly unscathed by the dramatic adventure. I'm still catching my breath when the handyman comes back inside—to get to work on the job he was actually hired for—and the other handyman, the one peeking out the window with me, says, "Why did you do that? It's just going to come back!" To which the first guy replies, nodding toward me, "Well, if you had caught it, you could have decided what to do with it. But you were in the kitchen screaming with her."

I thank both handymen profusely. If they hadn't been here, I would have bolted out the door, letting the rat have full run of the house until *anyone but me* could come catch it—whether that took hours, days, or weeks.

The small plywood landing in the attic is heavily sprinkled with rat poop. There are little rat footprints in the dust on the HVAC and ductwork, and the expanse of pink insulating fluff is full of tunnels—and maybe a colony of rat friends and rat relatives and rat babies. Sure, I now have a new, safe ladder to use to get up here to do what needs doing, but my courage to use it has been shaken. I hire a company to set traps and to fill the tiny holes through which the rats have snuck into my newly constructed house (in a neighborhood that was, not long ago, a big field, and is still under construction). For a week or so, I hear rustling in the wall behind my headboard, and I lie in bed, night after night, eyes wide open, wondering what I'll do if a rat or two make a sudden appearance. *Move out.* That's my alone-in-the-middle-of-the-night conclusion.

I've been well aware over these past several years that I miss the feeling of *safety in numbers*. But I miss the feeling of *comfort in numbers* (in numbers bigger than one), too.

I conquered the attic ladder's potential *I've fallen and can't get up* situation. I found an independent-feeling work-around solution. (Yay!) But the whole rat-falling-from-the-ceiling episode made me realize something: it's much easier to find ways to work around the practical and *safety* issues of living alone than it is to find ways to work around the *emptiness*—the great big hole where little displays of human comfort should be. The simple connection that makes things like *creatures with twitchy whiskers* seem less frightful or fraught with peril . . . or even makes things like that seem funny.

•

My eighty-seven-year-old mom and dad have been visiting for a few days, seeing my new life and house here in Texas. The last time they traveled by air, a few years ago, I was with them, so I was already aware they weren't going to be the confident travelers they once were. But after my older brother, Thomas, got them onto their plane for the trip here, he called me to emphasize that they are no longer able to navigate the airport on their own. At all. Dad lost the boarding passes several times, and they had to keep getting new ones, so Thomas recommended that, when the time comes, I hold all of their documents myself, in addition to guiding them all the way to their seats. I assured him I would get them safely onto their plane back to Minnesota.

Well, I've just dropped Mom and Dad off at the airport, and I feel like the worst daughter of the year. It has been pouring rain all morning, and all of the covered parking was full, so we (I) had a couple of less-than-ideal choices. We could go to the un-covered long-term parking lot and either walk back to the air-port (no) or get the shuttle (maneuvering Mom, Dad, and their luggage through the rain from the car to the place where the shuttle picks up its passengers, and then getting them and their luggage on—and off—that bumpy, wobbly shuttle once it finally arrived). Or I could drop them off for curbside service. We (I) picked curbside service from this short list of bad options. But, since Dad dismissed my suggestion of arranging some airport assistance, it meant that once they stepped inside the terminal, they would be on their own.

I pulled my car up to the weather-protected drop-off point, helped them to get checked in with the skycap, and watched as their luggage was tagged and tossed onto a towering pile before being rolled away on a cart. I asked if I could leave my car parked there for a while, given the circumstances, but was told no. So I gave Mom and Dad a bunch of instructions and reminders and hugs. And off they went.

Now, back in my car, still parked at the curb, I'm looking at the door through which my parents have just disappeared. I'm wondering if I should drive to the long-term parking lot, shuttle back to the airport as quickly as possible, and try to catch up with them. But as I run the whole scenario through my mind, I realize that since neither my parents nor their tickets would be with me, I wouldn't be allowed through airport security. And since Dad didn't bring his cell phone with him to Texas, I wouldn't be able to reach him to somehow make all this work. So Mom and Dad are navigating the airport on their own. And I'm hoping and praying they make it home safe and sound.

The version of events that my dad shared with me about their departure from Minnesota a few days ago was far different from the story my brother had shared. In Dad's version, the chaos and confusion were attributable to the airport and the people in it. So, since there are no other eyes watching over things today, I'm pretty sure we'll never know the truth of whatever actually happens.

While Mom and Dad were here, my younger brother, Jonathan, came from California to join the fun for a few days, too, leaving his wife and young son at home this trip so we could focus our time on our parents. We went for walks on the trails, enjoying Texas's summerlike autumn weather, ate at favorite local restaurants, and had a small dinner party with some neighborhood friends outside on the covered patio; Mom and Dad are quite vigorous, even as they're pushing ninety. Jonathan turned their fascination with my Roomba into a home movie by sticking his cellphone to its side with some tape, capturing my parents' amusement as it bumbled around doing its work, seemingly chasing them in the process. I'm happy I have that. I think Mom and Dad had wanted to see their daughter happy and settled in her new place—and they saw that. I think they left feeling at peace.

But my peace keeps being shaken.

My rug keeps being tugged.

Just as life started to feel like it was settling in, just as I was getting comfy, like I'd finally found my spot, Josh lost his job in New York City—a new pattern. Several months ago, he'd hinted that things might not be going too well there, and if things didn't work out, he would move back to DC to be with his new husband, so I can't say I'm surprised. Or that I wasn't forewarned. I just wish I hadn't ignored the signs pointing in the direction of where things were headed and allowed myself to believe I could peacefully begin landing. A landing that is now definitely not going to happen.

Long before he lost this job, Josh had invited me and a group of my friends to use the beach house he built in Delaware for several days—a luxurious rental property when not being used as his second home, but for us, purely a gift. Months later, when our girls' trip finally took place, Josh met us there the first night, showing us around, cooking us a scrumptious pasta dinner, giving us tips on where to eat, who could build us a bonfire on the beach, and where to find his reserved parking spot downtown. It was nice to spend a little time with Josh, the man I once lived for, but whom I hadn't seen for almost two years. A softening of any hard feelings remaining after the divorce.

The beach house was stunningly gorgeous. No detail had been overlooked, and every detail was perfect; Josh's husband is a spectacularly talented decorator. Every bedroom had a theme, and my friends and I took our time in choosing which one we wanted to claim as our own. Three crystal chandeliers hung above the dining-room table, and a cluster of huge old demijohns hung above the kitchen island—giant glass raindrops that were, in a previous life, used for storing Italian wine. The pool was in a courtyard with a cabana and rectangular fire table, and the living room could be opened to all of this by pushing back wall-to-wall, floor-to-ceiling patio doors, making one enormous indoor/outdoor room. Elegantly casual. Magnificently inviting. No wonder this house had been featured in home magazines and newspapers. It was a dream. And my friends and I were living it.

After such a lovely time, without my even being aware, my rug started to slowly drift and settle again. Everything was going to be okay. Josh was warm and friendly, boisterous and confident, and he didn't seem at all concerned about losing his job.

Several weeks later, Josh sent me a text:

Hi! I need to fill you in on what I'm planning to do professionally, it obviously impacts all of us money-wise but it's very exciting.

This is not good. Since the boys are financially independent of Josh, I will be the only one of "us" impacted by whatever exciting thing lies ahead for him. And money-wise, our only attachment is alimony.

After Josh sends me more information, I text him back:

The pitch is very intriguing. This will be quite an adventure and I'm happy for you and whatever lies ahead. But I'm hurt that you've even considered toying with my livelihood in order to pursue this exciting/sexy/glamorous new venture. I have tried to rebuild my life since the first time you pulled the rug out from under it, and I live life very carefully. I still drive my 2004 4-Runner, I'm committed to monthly payments for income tax, mortgage, property tax, health insurance, and all of the other expenses of life. I'm writing, hoping to earn enough money to someday be self-

sufficient, or even just get by, but, until then, I do what I do to help people in the same position that we're in—as well as to honor Joey. I'm hurt that the quality and stability of my life seems to be disposable when you are in pursuit of fulfilling your own dreams.

So, um, no.

Josh is like a helium balloon, bobbing merrily along, and I am like a lead weight. He's dragging me around—and I'm holding him back.

•

One of the best things about moving into a neighborhood where the houses are still being built is that all of the neighbors are newcomers, too, and so everyone here (at my super-friendly end of the street) is ready to make new friends. There are endless opportunities to plan little gatherings, which I love to do. Baby showers and ladies' night, Cinco de Mayo and Thanksgiving, and a progressive New Year's Eve dinner—a house-to-house roam, enjoying the next yummy course all the way until midnight. I like planning and decorating and cooking and hostessing the fun. And I like making events, both big and small, into something special—a birthday, a new job, a hard-earned good grade; celebrating life's events together, even if it's just with a hug and a favorite meal, is an invisible bond-builder.

But when my family disappeared, the most natural outlet for this sort of thing mostly disappeared with it.

Now, it's Christmas. *'Tis the season to be jolly.* The trees and the wreaths, the carols and the cookies, the bows and the tinsel and the stockings hung by the chimney with care. It's also my first Christmas without my boys. Both boys. Either boy. Rick is with his dad this year, which is only right (although choosing which parent to spend the holidays with isn't a choice kids, even adult kids, should be stuck having to make). And Joey, as he's been for so many years, is somewhere far away. This is the first time I've had to figure out how to do Christmas on my own.

Cindy said I should bring my jammies and walk across the street to spend Christmas Eve and morning with her family. And other friends called from afar to invite me to do the same thing. But as close as my friends and I may be, I'm not *truly* family, and I don't want to intrude. So when my dad bellowed heartily over the phone to "come spend Christmas with the old folks!" that's what I decided to do.

In the past, I would usually pull out the Christmas decorations and baking pans on the day after Thanksgiving and pack them all away on New Year's Day. Usually, I would enjoy basking in the sights, sounds, and aromas of the holiday for all those many weeks. But not this year. This year, I didn't decorate my house at all. No tree, no glitter, no sprinkles. There was no point, since no one was going to be there for the big day. There was also no point because the big, gaping hole in this holiday (in all holidays)—the one that has deepened with each year that Joey hasn't shown up—was now, with the divorce and a family scattered, sucked into a bigger, gaping black hole vortex, making the holiday, therefore, dead.

All I really want for Christmas is my boys at home with me. One small happy family. But that's not a gift I'm going to find under the tree this year. I don't like it, but I don't want to spend the holiday wallowing around in my miserableness, either. So, before heading to my mom and dad's house, I pull myself together. I remind myself of the reason for the season and keep my focus on that.

Together, we decorate their Christmas tree, placed in its usual spot in front of the living-room windows. Dad has trouble remembering where he stored the lights, and Mom keeps leaving the room and forgetting to come back, but I'm having fun hanging the old ornaments, especially the ones my two brothers and I made as kids out of Styrofoam and sequins and red and green construction paper and glue. We turn on some Christmas music, and Mom sways to the music and sings. Dad and I bake some cookies, do some Christmas shopping, and wrap some gifts. But maybe the best gift of all is that the unfolding of life's circumstances led me to be here. If things had gone as I'd originally hoped and planned, I'd be down in Texas with Rick, instead. But this is where I belong, spending this special time with my parents. Our time together is limited now, as their clocks are winding down.

Not everything here is as it should be. In fact, some things are the exact opposite of how they should (i.e., used to) be. Dad now does most of the cooking, and Mom now bosses him around to do this and that when she's not in bed. But there's great comfort in *family,* through all of its many seasons. A deep sense of belonging and eternalness. Family is life's warm, cozy security blanket. I hope my kids feel that, even though we're all thrown to the wind.

•

Joey's ear is caked in blood, and it appears that most of it is missing. I only know this because a friend saw the photo posted on Facebook and took the rare step of forwarding it to me, thinking an injury like this is something I should know about. I don't follow Joey on Facebook, although there was a time when I did. Well, I didn't just follow him; I stalked him—obsessively—not wanting to miss any posts before they were deleted, posts that might give me a hint of the truth of what might be going on. Eventually, I came to realize this wasn't healthy for either of us. I came to realize that I don't need to know about the things I can do nothing about and that my worrying helped no one. But, even so, there are still things I want to know about this son whom I love, and I still spend a lot of time worrying (and crying) on his behalf—it's just more of a simmering stew now than a rolling boil. And an occasional gusher instead of an endless flood. The umbilical connection is strong, and innate mom-feelings and -reactions are hard to contain, but compared to a few years ago, I've got my side of things under far more control.

I send Joey a text, saying *I love you, sweet son!* I don't mention his ear—while it was right for me to be made aware that he's been seemingly seriously injured, I don't need to get pulled into the whole trauma and drama and truth or lies around that. It has taken a long time for me to establish my boundaries. Boundaries meant to protect myself, not punish him. Boundaries that are firm but not rough. I don't expect a reply, since I haven't heard from him for months. My long string of calls and texts and silly emojis has been ignored, even the messages reminding him of my annual trip to Florida coming up in several months, in April, as always—to get (and give) a much-needed hug. I don't know why his communication dried up, but this has happened before, and then, one day, he's back, texting and calling. I'll keep sending him love till, hopefully, he comes back again.

I know there's nothing I can do to help Joey; not directly, anyway. Not with my hands all over his business, trying to fix things and redirect things and plug up the never-ending new holes in the damn leaky dam. I know this because I have lived and breathed trying to outmaneuver his disease for years. But that doesn't mean I'm sitting back and doing *nothing.* Instead, I'm letting my love and hope for him flow outward in ripples and waves—and I'm sure other moms are out there doing the same thing, too—hoping the ripple effect of mom-love will tumble along until it reaches the child I (we) cannot.

Before moving from Maryland to Texas, I passed the Bistro Boyz program into some very capable hands. It didn't take long, however, for me to miss it, and soon I was creating another project for cooking with at-risk teens here, this time at a Catholic maternity home. And this time, on my own (because keeping a bunch of women and teams organized adds a complicated layer to the whole adventure). This time, I'm keeping it simple. Once a week, on Thursday mornings, I arrive at the dorm kitchen around ten to start preparing a yummy lunch for the girls. Then I get things ready for midafternoon, when they return to start cooking dinner after finishing up their day of on-campus classes—the meats and spices, the cutting boards and mixer, the pots and pans and miscellaneous gadgets. There are usually about eight to twelve girls living here at any given time, and we have a couple of hours together before the young mamas go to collect their babies from the day care in the building right next door. The rest of the girls, the girls soon to give birth, stay with me to finish stirring sauces, checking whatever is baking in the oven, and setting the table. At five-thirty, there's a buzz of activity as the moms get their babies comfortably plopped into their high chairs and bouncers, and we all crowd around the table to eat what we've cooked. (Usually, it's quite delicious, even if it doesn't always look like the recipe's picture, but on occasion we've whipped up a total disaster.) Thursdays with the girls are very fun and chaotic and super-relaxed, all at the same time. Very *family.*

We've made chicken-and-waffle sandwiches, roasted vegetables of all kinds, and bread shaped like little bunnies—I want them to have the experience of making meals from fresh ingredients instead of from things that come in a box. We've made pressure-cooker pork ribs and some skin-on potato salad for the Fourth of July, and a turkey lattice-wrapped with bacon and a pecan pie for Thanksgiving. I cook with the girls the same way I cooked with my boys when they were young—not as a demonstration, but very hands-on. As we bump around in the kitchen together, these young girls are learning how to prepare healthy meals for their sprouting families, while enjoying the process. And I'm enjoying doing something to help them at a difficult time in their lives, while paying my love for Joey sideways.

Just as with *being addicted* or *being gay, being pregnant* as an unwed teen is highly stigmatized and judged. But what I see every Thursday is a bunch of girls—between the ages of twelve and seventeen—behaving like the children they are (in now very adult bodies), playing and laughing and crying while trying to figure out their new grown-up lives. As *children,* these girls responded to life's strongest drive, as nature, if not society, intended. (It's possible that some of the girls may have been raped; I don't know any details about any of their circumstances.) This Catholic maternity home was started as a way to take a difficult situation and make it better, not worse, by wrapping it in kindness—a wonderful example of *making a real difference.* The exact opposite result than what happens with harsh judgment.

•

I snore.

I know this because I've woken myself up a few times when no one else is around; no one toward whom I can point a no-*you*-did-it finger. Maybe I've always snored but was out-snored by Josh and our assorted dogs, but I think this is new. And it's things like this, along with the relentless invasion of pounds and wrinkles, that have me convinced I will never want to date. I can't imagine introducing this whole package to someone new. All at once. Instead of gradually, over the years, as marriage intended.

It's also hard to imagine introducing some unsuspecting soul to all of my family baggage over a get-to-know-you dinner. There's a lot of stigmatized material here for someone to grapple with—it's a struggle for even for my family and friends to understand things sometimes. It's hard to imagine some unsuspecting soul being happy that *I* was the one he chose to call for a date. Or getting a second call back.

At a friend's insistence, I did tiptoe into one of the dating websites for about five minutes. But it seemed to me there was an abundance of shirtless guys with names like *Adonis,* flexing their muscles while sitting on motorcycles—and so I skedaddled my way back out of there very fast. That world holds absolutely no interest for me. Basically, it's like *trying on* complete strangers ordered from a picture in a catalog and hoping for a fit. No thanks. I know how that process makes me feel with a mere swimsuit. So I know I don't have the stomach for that.

The last time I went on a date, I was in my twenties; I need to *take care* as I *take time* to rediscover who I am as *me* minus the *us.*

At this point in my life, Josh and I should have been rediscovering ourselves as empty nesters moving to life's next phase—I never expected that I'd be having to discover who I am on my own. For twenty-eight years, I was dancing in the dark, and I will not make that mistake again. I will take all the time I need to see what's really real and to see what I want and need. And as of right now, several years after our divorce, my heart is telling me that *I had my family; I only want one.* Even if that means being lonely. Right now, all I want is to be a mom, a daughter, a friend, a sister, and an author. (And, someday, a grandma. But I'm the only one who is ready for that yet.) I may or may not ever be ready to date.

But I am, more or less, doing just dandy on my own.

Even when things seem like they might not be figure-out-able, I'm slowly figuring them out. I've figured out how to install a screen door, mow the grass, take care of a rattlesnake situation in my backyard, and set stone blocks into cement to make a border around the garden at the front of my house. A friend of mine says I have *grit*. I guess I do. (Even if I can't deal with rats.) I guess I acquired some grit in the trauma of being the mom of an addicted child, and in the darker corners of India. But it didn't feel like grit then. It feels like grit *now* that I'm alone.

The last time Rick was here for a visit, I mentioned-hinted-suggested that he consider moving to Texas so we could be closer. Not a new conversation—he'd heard this before over the phone a few times. But I mentioned-hinted-suggested this again after we'd had a nice day at the movies and a dinner out—I like having him around. My twenty-six-year-old son replied, looking a little horrified, "Mom, do you know how hard it would be for me to move back home with you?" To which I replied back, probably also looking a little horrified, "No, I'm not inviting you to live in my *house*, just in my *state*!" The truth is, while I'd *love* to have Rick live nearby, I don't *need* him to live nearby. And there's a big difference between the two. It may not always be easy, but I can take care of myself, and I don't want him to think that I can't.

Finally, I'm no longer just dangling up in the air. My rug is coming in for a landing.

Part Two

Up the Decline

We're all
just walking each
other home.
—RAM DASS

4

The Old Folks

There's one thing this disease can't take away and
that is love. Love is not a memory—it's a feeling that
resides in your heart and soul.

—UNKNOWN

HONK! HONK HONK HONK! Without stopping for the red light
or the steady stream of oncoming traffic, Dad took a right turn at
a busy intersection. Riding in the back seat, I braced for impact
as the cars zooming toward me (in slow motion) swerved every
which way, brakes squealing. Seemingly unaware of the unfolding
chaos, Dad drove onward as angry honks and eyeballs followed us
down the road. Mom, calmly sitting next to him in the front passenger seat, said, "Do you hear all that whistling?" To which Dad
replied, "No." And on we went.

A near-death experience. And an *eye-opening* experience, too.

While in Golden Valley for Christmas recently, I finally ac-
knowledged what I've known (but not wanted to know) for quite
some time: my Dad is no longer able to drive safely. For his sake,
for my mom's sake, and for the sake of everyone else on the road,
something needs to be done.

My brothers and I have seen this day coming for years. We've
periodically discussed our concerns about Dad's driving and what
we should do about it, but each time we have settled on doing

nothing, none of us willing to put a big nail in his coffin. Mom hasn't driven for years—glaucoma has left her blind in one eye, and arthritis has left her hands quite crippled—so Dad's whole existence revolves around taking care of things: Mom, their house and yard, and life. He is a rolling stone, always busily and happily getting stuff done. Taking away his purpose, his ability to do the job that gives his life meaning, would kill him.

But now the long-dreaded time is here.

We don't want Dad's wonderful life to end on a note of avoidable tragedy (or behind bars), but he thinks his driving is fine, so he is not going to give up his car keys willingly. We also don't want to spend our waning years with Dad arguing, trying to convince him of what he doesn't want to believe, while hiding keys and car batteries. So we decide to reach out to the people who have the authority to make the hard decision for us—and make it stick.

I've been in this sort of situation before—accepting the impossibility of making someone do something they don't want to do—but also accepting the impossibility of just leaving it at that. And so, years ago, I wrote a letter to the judge presiding over one of Joey's court cases, without Joey knowing, on Joey's behalf: *It seems that an order from the court may be his only hope. It's terror for my son's life that has me leveraging this arrest to get him help before the inevitable, potentially fatal, fall. I'm pleading with you to force Joey to do time, a very long time, in rehab.*

Now, as then, I mail off another letter, bearing the toughest love of all:

Dear Driver and Vehicle Services,

I am concerned about my father's driving ability. My brothers and I will no longer be passengers in his car, nor will we allow our children to ride with him. He seems unaware of his reduced ability to react quickly and decisively to traffic conditions, even though he's had numerous near-miss accidents, has frequently lost his car in parking lots, gets confused with parking meters and kiosks, and has reported getting lost trying to get home on what should be familiar routes.

It is with a heavy heart that I'm requesting my father be assessed for at-risk driving; I understand the potential ramifications of this, but I also understand the potential ramifications if I do not.

Thank you.

It's not only Dad's driving that had (seemingly) suddenly crossed a threshold. I noticed a lot of other things during my holiday trip, too—but I'm not sure if this means that Mom and Dad, at age eighty-eight, have suddenly, dramatically aged, or if it means I have scratched through yet another layer of denial (of which I seem to have many) and was finally able to see what I hadn't wanted to see.

Mom slept a lot. And she didn't leave the house at all. This is supposedly due to bladder issues (although she doesn't run to the bathroom any more frequently than me and half my friends) and vertigo, something she's suffered with on and off the past several years (although my brothers and I have never seen any signs of dizziness or adverse reactions to motion). As always, when Mom was up and about, she seemed fine, easily turning and bending, only mentioning vertigo as a reason to go back to bed or to avoid going out anywhere. But even so, Dad kept a glass bowl full of loose Dramamine pills on the kitchen counter for her to take as needed (easy access for her crippled hands). I told him I don't think Mom has vertigo or that Dramamine is meant to be available by the bowlful, and that I'm pretty sure this medication is meant to be used only for short-term motion sickness. But what do I know? I'm not the doctor—*he is*.

I suspect that vertigo and bladder issues are Mom's way of isolating herself because she's aware, at some level, that her cognitive abilities have been slipping, and she finds safety and comfort in keeping her world small. And I think she has come to believe that she really has these ailments, even if there are no signs of either. Vertigo is her go-to rationale for asking Dad to keep her friends at bay and cancel her various appointments, and I could see this had been going on for quite a while—her usually short, snow-white locks were shoulder-length, so she hadn't even been out to go to the salon.

Mom doesn't like her hair long; she commented on it every day, but I couldn't convince her to let me take her out for a haircut. So I placed one of the wooden kitchen chairs in the middle of the family room, wrapped Mom's shoulders in a big towel—dampening her hair with a spray bottle since she said her vertigo was too extreme to take a shower—and I cut her hair, for the first time ever. She closed her eyes and sat very still as I gently pulled the brush through her hair and snipped away. Whenever I paused to check my not-so-handy handiwork, she would say some version of *this feels so good, keep going,* and so I did. The longest, most beautiful haircutting session in the history of haircutting, I'm sure. (And the actual cut turned out okay, too.)

With newly opened eyes, I watched Mom go up and down the tightly curving staircase, stairs that end in a slate foyer. But confident and nimble, she said she's doing fine holding on to the wooden banister with her crippled hands and navigating the sharp corners in her loose-fitting-but-favorite sheepskin slippers. At my insistence, she agreed to ask her doctor about getting an "I've Fallen and Can't Get Up" button; I know this isn't a solution for a fall down the stairs, but it would be peace of mind in case of other, lesser falls. Mom has always been small, but she has become smaller over the years. I can now rest my chin on the top of her head when I give her a hug, and she feels very frail, like a crystal candlestick that would easily break.

Dad is a bit more stooped than he used to be, but he still shovels the sidewalk in the winter, mows the yard in the summer, and almost always walks 10,000 steps a day; physically, he's quite vigorous. He does most of the cooking and cleaning now, having taken over what were Mom's jobs since forever, and he has even taken up ironing instead of going around wrinkly—or completely changing his *look,* which is pressed khakis and a tucked-in button-down shirt, worn with a belt and rugged brown leather shoes. I did notice an increased confusion about some things, though, like what button to push to turn on his computer—which probably explains why his regular morning emails to me are now less regular—and what button to push to turn the answering machine back on after someone keeps turning it off. I pulled Dad's cell phone out of the den cupboard, where he keeps it put away, telling him to charge it up, keep it charged up, and keep it with him wherever he goes, reminding him that we kids need to be able to reach him—and he needs to be able to reach us—whenever needed. But my brothers and I have said all of this before; Dad just isn't comfortable using a cell phone, and I'm pretty sure that as soon as I left, he shoved it back in the cupboard.

One day, Dad called me *Mom* after something I said or did crossed a boundary: "Thanks, *Mom.*" My help must not have seemed very helpful to him since his tone on the word *Mom* was pretty sharp. I must have been treating Dad like a child—incapable of doing, thinking, or being something quite right—after a lifetime of being very capable, indeed. I need to be more careful in walking the invisible line between help and interference, safety and independence, pride and control. This is Mom and Dad's twilight stroll, not mine.

It seems like Mom and Dad are happy and doing okay living on their own in their house, together, as they've done for over five decades. And as they've always hoped to do all the way to the end. My older brother, Thomas, lives just ten minutes away and keeps an eye on things, helping our parents out whenever needed, as he always has, even with a full-time job and two now-teenage kids. But now, increasingly, *keeping an eye on things* and *helping out* is transitioning to a different level, and, therefore, so am I. Fortunately, as an author, I can work from anywhere, so I'll be able to travel back to Golden Valley whenever my parents might need or want me.

December in Texas is much warmer than in Minnesota; now that I'm back home, I'm wearing a short-sleeved shirt while puttering around in the garden rather than shivering in temperatures far below zero and trying not to slip while waddling rapidly across parking lots like ice rinks. It's about one hundred degrees colder there than here (!). The plants grow fast here at home, so I'm pulling weeds and trimming the errant green shoots that have become unruly during my week up north. This is therapy for me, being outside in the sunshine and flowers, taming nature's bounty into beauty. As I begin trimming the wisteria, its vines twisting and curling around the beams on the wooden arbor and giving shade to my back patio, I'm thinking about my parents and the future, about what might be coming next, but slowly, slowly, I drift into thinking about my parents and the past . . .

The old folks. That's how Dad has referred to himself and Mom since before they were actually old folks, at least from my current perspective. But the way he says it, it's always wrapped in a smile.

When Dad says, "Come visit the old folks!" it's to the same tune as "Let's have some fun!" I started calling him Pops or Big Daddy in the past several years, which is not something I could have gotten away with when I was in my teens, but he beams when I say it now.

Dad enlisted in the Navy the day he graduated from high school, which led to him serving as a corpsman on a hospital ship in WWII, then to medical school, and then, about sixty years ago, to meeting my mom, a nurse at the hospital where he was completing his doctor's residency. When I was growing up, it seemed he was always at the hospital taking care of patients, but in my memories, he was also home to eat dinner with the family every night (after sharing a long, silent, swaying hug with my mom), at every school event, and there carving the turkey every Thanksgiving and helping to decorate the tree every Christmas. As the years went on, as his on-call schedule eased up and he had more time, Dad took up woodworking. His first project was a *floor harp* (not a birdhouse or cutting board), followed by a curly maple harpsichord—a plucked-string instrument that resembles a longer and narrower grand piano. Once Dad got the idea, once the woodworking bee started buzzing around in his bonnet, he bought some books and figured out how to do what he wanted to do, a trait he passed on to me and my brothers; like Dad, we *think we can* and so we *do.*

Careful with his words, Dad doesn't talk much about his inner workings, but one day he told me something that opened my eyes to a nice new way of doing things:

My dad once told me that he thanked God every morning for all the good in his life rather than asking God for something more. Until I heard my dad's words, I'd been a greedy little asker, but I've found the thankful approach to be far more satisfying. There are no disappointments, and there's no better way to start the day than with a heart-load of gratitude, especially on a day that turns sour.

I don't always remember to start the day being thankful —especially when I'm busy rushing around for a strong cup of coffee, a hair dryer, and something that fits—but, when I do remember, it's possible I may glow until noon.

Positive thinking works so well for me in the morning, I've decided to start doing something similar each night before going to sleep. Once my head hits the pillow, I will start mining the day for something good on which to focus. It might be just the thing I need to fend off the midnight monsters that keep me awake. I'm going to think of one good thing from my day and hang on to it. Then I'm going to carry it into my dreams.

—*Tending Dandelions,* 198

He also watches his words in moments of frustration or anger; through all the years and everything they've brought with them— three kids, crazy drivers, spilled milk—I've never heard Dad swear, not even *damn* or *H-E-double-toothpicks* (the choice words that Mom occasionally lets loose).

Sweet, sweet Mom—she doesn't have a mean or crabby bone in her body. Quiet but strong, she is guided by (and has guided her family by) the simple principles of *if you don't have something nice to say, don't say anything.* And *do unto others as you would have them do unto you.* And *the world would be really boring if everyone thought and did and liked the same thing.* And *just follow the Ten Commandments.* There was no gossip in our house. Mom liked to say, "Great minds discuss ideas and average minds discuss events, but small minds discuss people," so I was raised without even a hint of mean-spirited (or mean-girl-spirit) vibes. Since forever, and in her own subtle way, Mom let it be known that I should never accept being treated badly by anyone, that a spouse should also be a best friend, and that I could be and do anything I set my heart and mind to, giving me a foundation of strength I'm only now fully recognizing.

Mom loves to dance and sing and play the piano. I remember coming home from school to find her standing at the sink washing dishes while belting out some opera tune in a soprano vibrato, or sitting at the piano in the living room, pounding out a song she heard on the radio, playing by ear. The rest of us are musical clods, in all ways—no rhythm, no voice, no nothing—although we all tried. Her other artistic talents, however—like painting and drawing—she did, fortunately, pass on.

Mom and Dad believed that education was the best gift they could give my brothers and me, both schoolwise and lifewise; they paid for our college, and they allowed us to learn from our mistakes—by facing the consequences—rather than trying to control things when we messed up. They believed in hands-on helping the folks who need helping, something they did every day in their chosen medical professions, but also in their volunteer work, like when they went to rural hospitals in Taiwan and Africa for several years. They believed in *getting along*; I've never seen Mom and Dad argue or bicker, and I've never seen signs of hostilities on a slow burn or heard them reply to one another with snappy snark. This doesn't mean they always agreed on things; it just means they kept their private business private, tried to do the right thing for themselves and each other, and didn't add trouble to the troubles life already brings. They believed in honesty, in both their words and their actions, so I never knew anything different. And they believed in *not butting in* unless asked and in *biting their tongue* even when faced with things they didn't understand—like my son's addiction, my husband's gayness, and my divorce.

Now, some parts of the essence of Mom and Dad are fading and changing. Some parts of them I may never see again. But no matter what happens next, I will carry more than a lifetime of memories made in a world where I was happy, loved, and safe—I will also, still and forever, carry their humility and integrity, their wisdom and strength. *Their* essence is hopefully a part of *my* essence.

An essence, hopefully, projected to my boys before our family became so broken. And still.

·

In the month since Christmas, I've start working on a new manuscript—*Tending Dandelions: Honest Meditations for Mothers with Addicted Children.* I picture it as a small (but mighty) book, something moms can easily tuck into a purse or fit on their nightstand. I'm trying to paint poignant vignettes with my words, touching upon all aspects of addiction from a mother's point of view—a mother whose child isn't in recovery, a mother who continues to navigate the endless road of Letting Go, a mother who's trying (but not always succeeding) to move forward with strength and grace. I'm filling it with a mother's hard-learned lessons, from denial to acceptance to inner peace, including this one (page 165): *The hardest thing I've ever done is to acknowledge that I can't control my son's addiction or recovery—but maybe the most important thing I've ever done is to let recovery begin with me.*

Joey is unaware that I'm working on a new book. For years, we've avoided talking about anything having to do with addiction at all, and *Tending Dandelions* isn't really about him—it's about a mom finding her way to healing in the place where love and addiction meet—but still, I want to tell him about what I'm up to; I want to let him know that I'm still working on trying to change the way addiction is perceived, for him. But Joey has been incommunicado, unresponsive to my attempts at reaching out, for almost a year. I want him to know that I love him and miss him so much.

> "Mom." *Sometimes a whisper will wake me up late at night.* "Mom." *It sounds just like my son, in his no-longer-a-child voice. I can almost feel his breath as he leans in, speaking softly in my ear, but when I open my eyes, he's not really standing at my bedside. He is not there, like when he was little, needing help in the dark of night.*
>
> *But the umbilical connection is forever. Maybe, wherever he is, my son is in trouble. Maybe he needs me or wants his mom's comfort, and maybe I'm feeling that need. I can only hope that he feels the love I send back along the same path.*
>
> *Sometimes I still have dreams about the child I rarely see and hardly know at all. Some are fuzzily pleasant, while others are vivid nightmares. But, either way, we get to spend some rare and unexpected time together.*
>
> *A hug. A laugh. A walk in the park. A whisper.* "Mom."
>
> *Dreams. It's as if sometimes our souls still need to touch.*
>
> —*Tending Dandelions,* 111

For better or worse (and there's definitely a lot of both), the letter I wrote to the DVS about Dad's driving achieved its goal; they summoned him for driving and cognition tests, he failed both, and his license has been revoked. Over the phone, Dad sounded pragmatic, flummoxed, and depressed—all at once—and he's very aware that life as he's known it is over.

Thomas, Jonathan, and I have been discussing different options for Dad to use in getting around town, but there is no perfect solution. Since Dad doesn't like using a cell phone, the Uber app won't work. Neither will the ride services that require making plans several days ahead, even though they take appointments via the phone—he needs more spontaneity than that. We got a hard *no* from Dad at the suggestion of trying Metro Mobility, a bus service for people unable to manage using regular city buses—he won't even consider that. And Dad's preference, getting rides from friends, isn't something he can count on, even if that's the most comfortable-seeming option. So, for now, taking a taxi is going to be his new means of transportation. Dad is worried about the cost—$15 each way to his Swedish woodcarving class—but we've assured him he doesn't need to worry; the expense of his outings will be far less than the expenses of owning and maintaining a car. And Thomas will pick him up for a weekly errand and grocery-shopping trip, so the essential outings will be taken care of.

When talking with Dad, I mention the benefits of getting on the waiting lists of some assisted-living places, something I've been reluctant to bring up again after a negative response a few years ago. But now, since he's no longer able to drive, I think this idea might seem more appealing. He says he doesn't want to be pushed. I follow up with an email, anyway. Pushing a bit.

Dear Mom and Dad,

I'm following up on our call to encourage you to please *get yourselves on the waiting list of an assisted living place that you like. You may never need it, but life throws unexpected curveballs. I know this is something we'd all rather pretend isn't a possibility,* but it is. *And we kids don't want to have to "settle" in regard to your care because we haven't planned ahead and then no good options are available when we might need them.*

Moving to Texas is an option; I'd love to have you close by, but you need to decide if that's something you'd even consider—you need to decide if you're willing to leave behind your life connections or if you'd rather stay in Minnesota. You need to think about and talk about what you want.

I know I speak for Thomas and Jonathan when I say we want what is best for you, but the time has come for you to decide what that is. We will help you in any way that we can. We can be extra sets of eyes or ears or internet sleuths. Just ask.

You need to make a plan so that we don't have to blindly make decisions for you.

Loads of love,
Sandy

•

Thomas just discovered that Mom and Dad have been scammed. Apparently, what started as a garbage disposal issue ended with their main breaker box—the point where all the electricity comes into the house—being replaced at a cost of $6,000. Thomas reminded Dad that the breaker box had been replaced a few years before—maybe even by the same people. (And maybe it didn't need to be replaced then, either.) And a few weeks ago, Mom was very upset by a phone call they received, something about Joey, and she thought he was in trouble or danger. My guess is that it was a collection agency trying to track down Joey's money; I get those calls all the time, and they are intimidating. But who knows? Mom and Dad are targets for unsavory characters with their bags full of dirty tricks, and as much as we kids have tried to make them aware of some things to look out for, they forget. So we feel pretty helpless in protecting them from the bad guys.

But sometimes there's a *good* guy. Last year, Dad had their house painted, using the same painter he's used for decades. Dad kept writing him checks, not understanding that he'd paid the full amount for the job, twice. The painter—who could've just kept this windfall of extra money, or could've just torn the extra checks up—took the time to drive to Dad's bank and tell them that Dad is vulnerable to being taken advantage of. I would never have known about this lapse or the kindness that followed, except that Dad and I use the same bank brand, which somehow led them to me. So there was a chain of good guys, a chain of good people making the effort to do the right thing.

There's been a lot of confusion about doctor appointments lately—Mom refusing to go; Mom agreeing to go, but then Mom and Dad mistakenly go to the wrong address; calls from their doctors' offices telling them they've missed appointments (that they forget they made). So I asked Dad for their doctors' names and phone numbers to help sort things out. I actually already have this info, I copied it from the magnets on their refrigerator while I was there in December, *just in case,* but he needed to give permission for me to speak with them if I was going to have meaningful conversations, and he did. I shared with both doctors the issues my brothers and I are concerned about—Mom's "vertigo," excessive sleeping, cognitive decline, and weight loss; Dad's driver's license being revoked, his social isolation in taking care of Mom, his vulnerability to scams; the pros and cons of assisted living for them both. Their primary care doctors were able to line up a bunch of appointments for Mom and Dad for the next week, and I went back up to snowy Minnesota to make sure they got there. This is where I can be the most help to Thomas, I think, since he can't keep taking days off work.

Now, at the end of a busy, sad, frustrating, and worrisome week with Mom and Dad, I email my brothers before heading home. Although we've been communicating all along, getting everything written out helps keep everyone on the same page without a bunch of confusion (on top of what is already confusing):

Thomas and Jonathan, here's the scoop—

Doctor appointments for the folks were yesterday morning— I went in with Mom. She weighs eighty pounds, has lost seven pounds in the past year, and is obviously far too thin, with no reserves if she becomes ill. They did assorted cognitive tests, ending with the doctor telling her she has early dementia.

Vertigo has finally, officially been ruled out—as has anything more serious than basic overactive bladder, the other frequent complaint. The doctor was very clear in telling Mom that the only thing keeping her home, isolated, and sleeping is desire. She also said that all of this is symptomatic of dementia, and moving to an assisted-living place might help Mom to socialize and eat more. I'm glad I was in there because Mom completely misrepresented her lifestyle as physically active, social, and busy, etc.

After Dad had his physical, his doctor popped into Mom's examining room to ask me to join them next door for a chat. Dad's doctor has recommended a more comprehensive cognitive exam to determine if Dad has dementia, saying that smart, active people like him are able to cover their dementia better and longer than other people. Unfortunately, the first available appointment isn't for two months—until April. It would have been nice to get this all wrapped up while I'm here.

The doctor brought up the overpayment to the house painter (I had told him about this on the phone when we talked), and I brought up the $6,000 garbage disposal con. After discussing these incidents a bit, he, like Mom's doctor, also suggested they get on an assisted-living list now, and Dad agreed.

We then took Mom for an MRI to rule out some other unlikely cause for her dementia. She told the nurse she was there for her vertigo when we were checking in, and Dad wrote that on the form, too, so the reality of everything they had just learned about dementia and vertigo was ignored for the moment. On the ride home, however, Mom was quite angry about it all, telling Dad that she performed perfectly on the cognitive test, that she *does* have vertigo, and that her doctor is crazy. Dad made it clear that he doesn't like his doctor anymore, either, so I don't know if they will ever return to—or listen to—those doctors again.

We got the report from the MRI this afternoon, stating that Mom has brain shrinkage, which is consistent with dementia, and there are no signs of other factors that might cause it.

Early this morning, Mom had an ultrasound to check her liver, which was flagged from her lab work. Our plan was to then go for breakfast and look at a couple of assisted-living places, but we only made it to one, and Mom didn't go with us; after her ultrasound, she said she had vertigo and needed *to go home. The people at Sunshine Place gave Dad and me a nice tour, they were friendly, and Dad liked it, so once we learned there's a two-year wait for a two-bedroom assisted-living apartment, we made a refundable deposit to get Mom and Dad on the list. We can still look at other facilities, too, and we'll probably need to make multiple refundable deposits. Dad would be far less alone in a place like this than he is at home—the resident community seemed vibrant and welcoming, and he could have a social life again. At dinner, we talked about all of this with Mom—her response was to say that I had it all wrong, that Dad and I didn't sign up for both of them to move, that we had signed up for only her to move if Dad were to die first. I didn't correct her.*

Sunshine Place does not take Medicare, so we really need to know about Mom and Dad's finances. The two-bedroom assisted-living apartment, which includes meals and some home health care, is over $7,000 a month—and will only become more expensive as their needs increase.

I think the time has come to push for Thomas to be made the Power of Attorney on their finances and health care directives. As Mom and Dad told us ages ago, they wanted to make this change when the time came—they just aren't aware that that time has arrived. Mom is no longer able to make important decisions—she shouldn't be the one legally in charge of making health decisions for Dad—and Dad doesn't have a clear understanding of Mom's health issues or their finances. I've seen Dad keep shuffling around stacks of papers over here, but nothing looks very organized, and I'm not confident he's paying his bills (he says he is, but wouldn't let me take a look). If Thomas could oversee things, it would prevent delinquent bills, lessen the chances of a major scam, and give us a true understanding of what exactly they can afford as far as assisted-living places—and for how long. Right now, we're just guessing. I talked with Dad about all this. We dug out the Power of Attorney and living will documents, printed them out, and I stuck Post-it Notes on the parts I think should be updated—but he was overwhelmed. And I got the impression I've crossed as many butting-in boundaries as I can with him on this trip. Maybe you guys could explain to Dad why this is an important change to make when you talk to him next?

I print out a summary of what Mom's doctor said and hang it on the cabinet near the phone in the kitchen so Dad will see it and remember:

- As per her doctor, Mom does not have vertigo or life-altering bladder issues.
- Mom has early dementia, but increasing her activity level might help to slow down the process and will enhance her life.
- Mom can take a morning and an afternoon nap, but wake her after an hour each time. She doesn't need to sleep eighteen hours a day.
- Try to get Mom out of the house daily, even if it's just for a walk around the neighborhood.
- If Mom says she can't go somewhere because of vertigo or bladder issues, remind her that the doctor said she doesn't have that, so she can, in fact, go anywhere.

Thinking back, I'm not sure when things started changing with Mom and Dad; I'm not sure when what was *real* and what I *thought was real* forked off into two different directions. But I do remember they canceled their trip to see my new condo in Maryland because Mom had vertigo (and I just believed what I was told), so that red herring has been around for at least four years. And a year or two before that, I remember Dad having trouble counting out cash to pay for a bagel and coffee, and I was uncertain how long I should wait before stepping in to help. Maybe I've been too preoccupied with my worries about Joey and Josh and Rick to see the changes happening. Or maybe I've been subconsciously accepting nature's changes *without staring*. Or maybe I've been unable to see the changes, so small and gradual they've been like sporadic drops of rain into an ocean. Honestly, I don't know. But I see the changes, the reality, now. And I'm really grateful Mom and Dad visited me in Texas when they could because I don't think they'll be leaving Minnesota ever again.

·

In recent weeks, Dad has made it clear that he is his own man. He called to say he canceled the appointment we made while I was there a few months ago—the one where a specialist was going to do an assessment for dementia. Dad decided he didn't need it. He also said that Mom's vertigo seems a little better, and they might go to the arboretum to walk around and look at the soon-to-be-blooming flowers. And he said that he walks to his barber and the hardware store rather than taking a taxi, crossing a busy highway and walking about one mile each way (without sidewalks). No matter what we say, Dad is doing and believing what he wants to do and believe—including his risky jaunts around Golden Valley—and my brothers and I can't stop him.

I took my annual spring trip to Florida to see Joey—but I didn't see him. I'm not surprised things turned out this way, since he hadn't responded to any of my messages, but my heart is still aching. I'd been cautiously hopeful, because last year when I was there he didn't respond until the very last day—I just kept sending messages letting Joey know I was nearby at the hotel pool or a restaurant or a coffee shop so he could join me wherever, whenever, until finally he did. But this year *he didn't*.

The silence is too loud. Say something. *Please.*

I don't understand why I haven't been able to help you, to touch something in you with my love—or why nothing I have said or done has been able to match the power of the demon that holds you so tight, swatting away any hand that attempts to reach you. I don't understand the pull of the demon that's been leading you away from the people, places, and things that should be meaningful to you—and through torments that you shouldn't want to bear.

There's such agony in not knowing if you're alive. Or safe. Or a little bit happy. In not knowing if you've forgotten that you are loved. There's such agony in the silence. The silence has dragged on for longer than my heart can bear. I don't want to give up on you, on believing in you, on believing you will find your way back. But sometimes I do. Sometimes I give up on us both.

Say something. *Anything. One word on which to hang my hope that things will get better.*

—*Tending Dandelions,* 112

I keep trying to fill the hole in my life where Joey should be by doing speaking events and interviews, and I will even be filmed for a documentary in a few months—anything to keep the light shining on the disease of addiction. And to keep turning my pain, my love, into purpose.

I'm struggling, though. What do I do now, now that most of the people I've loved the most—the people who've been my *life*—I'm no longer able to connect with?

Trying to fill another hole, of which there are so many, I reach out to Josh. He still hasn't found a job, which must be as scary for him as it is for me. I send him a text:

> *I'm so sorry to learn about the shooting at the club in Orlando, and about the judgment and hatred so poised to strike in our world. But I'm grateful you are surrounded by a community of people who are accepting of what too many don't understand isn't theirs to judge. I'm working on reservations for a Philly/DC speaking trip at the end of September. I'd like to spend some time with you—more than just dinner, a real talk. I'd like to try again to find a new "us." Do you have room in your calendar? I need to book flights soon.*

Weeks later, Josh replies (ignoring what I feel was the most important part of my message): *Have you finalized your September plans? I'm mostly free but going to Florida the 22nd through 26th.*

Me: *Sorry, never heard from you so booked my travel schedule about a month ago. I'm in DC the 23rd and 24th.*

Josh: *That's too bad. I'm organizing a family reunion with my siblings and the kids in Florida.*

Months later, Josh sends his next text: *Give me a call sometime to catch up! And I hope you can reconsider taking a day or two to come to Florida the weekend of September 23rd. Big house on the beach. Both Ricky and Joey are coming.*

Me: *You scheduled the reunion for the same time I'm in DC, remember?*

Josh: *Ugh, I know. I had no choice as I had to work on the weekends before and after.*

I feel foolish, yet again. Thinking I can make things be something they are not. I can't fill a hole with more emptiness. I once heard a Maya Angelou quote: *When people show you who they are, believe them.* Okay. Finally. Really. I'm believing.

It's almost too much for my heart to handle once I realize how I must protect it from *two out of three* of my supposedly forever family:

> *My brain and my heart need to have a little chat. A meeting of the minds, so to speak. A tête-à-tête. They're not seeing eye-to-eye on how to ~~love a child suffering with addiction~~* **have a relationship with the father of my children.** *They can't agree on how to proceed.*
>
> *My heart, you see, is a bit like a battered wife. It keeps taking abuse and then taking the abuser back. Bludgeoned, bleeding, and bandaged, it continues to open the door—to trust, to believe, whatever ~~the addicted child~~ **the man who once loved me** says and does. Even after all it's been through. Because maybe, just maybe,* this time *will be different. Maybe this time my heart won't be crushed.*
>
> *My brain, on the other hand, says (as it's nursing my heart back to health), "When will you learn? Enough is enough. The heart is not a punching bag. The destructive cycle must stop. There comes a time when you've done all you can. A time when you must step back."*
>
> *My brain and my heart need to have a little chat.*
>
> —*"Tête-à-Tête," Readings for Moms of Addicts*

Over the past months, it seems the Dramamine Situation at Mom and Dad's house has gotten out of control. Well, even more out of control than usual. Dad says Mom is now taking about fifty pills a week (!!!) for her (nonexistent) vertigo, and she's very demanding that he keep her pill bowl well stocked. Thomas won't let Dad sneak any Dramamine into the grocery cart on their weekly shopping trips, so Dad has obviously been taking a taxi, or walking, to the store to keep the supply flowing. The pressure he's getting from Mom is stronger than the pressure he's getting from us kids to stop doing this pill thing—which is hard to imagine, since she is hardly scary. We're never sure what to believe anymore, so Thomas looked around the house and found enough boxes of Dramamine, both full and empty, that *fifty pills a week* could actually be happening.

I called Mom's doctor. She said taking this quantity of Dramamine could cause all kinds of bad side effects, including excessive sleeping, confusion, aggressiveness, and damage to Mom's liver and kidneys, some of which we are already seeing in her behavior and lab tests. We made an appointment for Mom for next month, in late October, so I'll go back up to Minnesota for that, and to see how she and Dad are doing while living with them for a few days, compared to how they were doing when I was there for a quick weekend in June.

When I talked to Dad, I told him we're going to put an end to the Dramamine Situation, adding, "When I get there in a few weeks, I'm going to be bossy." Dad replied, "You already are." I hate being in this position. I'm not confrontational by nature. And I hate pushing my help on someone who doesn't understand that they need it—I've had to do this with Joey, and it was never well received. But Thomas and I agree that this job falls to me. Thomas needs to continue on with his usual reassuring and trusted presence over the next few weeks—we don't want Dad to feel pressured from all sides.

Several months ago, I sent my *Tending Dandelions* manuscript off to Hazelden Publishing to see if it sparked any interest. And then several weeks later, I received a call from them saying YES! It will be published as part of their renowned meditation series— the first book of the series written specifically for moms who love a child doing battle with the disease of addiction. They also asked me to write an accompanying app to be titled *Readings for Moms of Addicts.*

Well, I've been working on both manuscripts for the past few months, polishing up my thoughts and words until they're just right, and I am finally done. I'm sending them off to the publisher, who will bring them to life.

Helping other moms living in the place where love and addiction meet—my mission, my purpose, my passion—now has wings.

Eager to get moving after a whole lot of sitting, I look around at my house, at all the things that have gone undone while I was busy writing, and I start digging in. I've done only the essentials for longer than I'd like to admit, so I have a big job ahead. Thank goodness for my fondness for reclaimed wood furniture, all weathered and warped—the table, sideboard, and nightstands can go (exactly) three weeks without showing the dust. This spring-cleaning-in-the-fall project is a good transition for me, moving from living inside of myself back to the real world. Moving from darkness to light. Writing about all the thoughts and feelings and realities of loving a child with addiction—revisiting the memories, the sadness, the fears, and the great big hole—is too deep to dip in and out of every day, so I tend to live in that place until the writing is done, taking brief chunks of time off once in a while to heal a bit before immersing myself once again. It's the only way I can find the stuff that is *real*.

I'm busily trying to capture a bunch of runaway dust bunnies when I get a text from Thomas: *Can you call Dad? He thinks Mom needs to go to a place where she can be cared for. He says she's getting argumentative and irrational. I've noticed a big decline lately, too.*

After calling Dad, I reply to Thomas: *We talked. I'm going to call Sunshine Place tomorrow to see if they might have a one-bedroom unit available for Mom. Dad isn't ready to commit to anything yet, but said Mom is getting "grumpy"—for example, she doesn't like what he cooks and storms off mad during dinner, and she has hit him. He sounded tired. This is completely out of character for her—I wonder if this rapid change is her dementia? Or if it's all the Dramamine he's been giving her? And I wondered that out loud to him, too. I told him to throw out all the Dramamine and to not buy any more, and if she comes looking for it, to avoid an argument, he could say he doesn't know where she put it.*

I go back to my cleaning, trying to scrub away so many feelings from so many angles, until I'm exhausted. First thing in the morning, I call Sunshine Place, then Dad. And then I send Thomas a text: *Sunshine Place said they had an opening for Mom, but that we would need to decide right away. When I called Dad to tell him the unbelievably lucky news, though, he said NO. "Everything is fine." So I called them back to say we don't need a place yet, after all. There might be another unit available in November, but, if so, they will need to work through the wait list, and it may be taken before getting to us.*

Clean, clean, clean, scrub, scrub, scrub. Sleep. Wake. Stretch. My cell phone rings. It's Dad.

I text Thomas: *Dad called a few minutes ago. He was kind of panicky, wants me to check with Sunshine Place again, doesn't recall* that we had this same conversation yesterday and that he declined the opening they had for Mom. He said he hides the deadbolt house keys now out of fear that she might wander outside and that he's afraid she'll leave water running or gas on when she roams the house at night.

More cleaning, more scrubbing. Sleep. Wake. Stretch.

My cell phone rings. It's Dad, but I don't answer it quickly enough.

I text Thomas: *I just missed a call from Dad, he left a message. He wants to talk about Mom, said he has "information that has never been shared before." I think she has a brain tumor—that would explain all this behavior, right? I'm thinking I might offer to go up there sooner rather than later and stay about a week. What do you think?*

Thomas: *I've suspected he's holding back information lately. Give it some thought after your conversation with him, but it does sound like it might be best to get here sooner.*

Me, a few hours later: *I don't know what's going on over there. The answering machine is now turned off so I can't leave any more messages, and somebody, eventually, picked up the ringing phone and hung right up on me. Twice. Not even a split second for me to say a word.*

Thomas: *I'll stop by on my way home from work.*

Me: *Things don't feel right—I'm just going to change my original flight from the end of October to now, will stay with them for a few days and assess things. My plan is to arrive the day after tomorrow, on Friday, October 7, and depart the following Wednesday, depending on how things go.*

Thomas: *I just stopped by the house. Mom answered the door, she carried on a conversation but was really mixed up. Two weeks ago she seemed pretty fine, and Dad seemed to be managing things.*

But last week things started to change. Whatever is happening is happening quickly.

Me, a few hours later: *I just talked to Dad. He had no recollection of leaving a voicemail this morning, said everything over there is fine. I reminded him that he'd said there was something he wanted to tell me about Mom, but he said she was in the room and so couldn't talk, but that it was nothing urgent. I told him I'm going to be there on Friday and that we will find an assisted living place for Mom, or at least get her on as many short waiting lists as possible. He said she will be mad and started talking about the weather.*

I think Dad reaches out for help when he's frightened by something Mom just did—something so disturbing that he wants us kids to save him. Save *them*. He knows he's in over his head. But then, later, he forgets. Or wants to forget, once whatever has happened has passed. But I need to pay attention to—I need to *honor*—the part of Dad that is asking for help. Even if that part soon disappears.

I don't know what's happening up in Minnesota, but I'm going to find out.

5

Goodbye, House

I'm just tired;
I just want the world to be quiet for a bit.

—MATTY HEALY

THOMAS: *HEADS UP: Mom just called, asking if I would call and tell you to cancel your trip. She said she lost your number. And something about rescheduling your visit till the weather is better. I said you're already on your way. Dad must have told her you're coming and what you're coming for.*

Me: *I just landed. There are seven voicemails from Mom, two of which are about the weather, and in the other five she doesn't say anything at all. I think you're right, Dad probably told her about the plan to look at assisted living places for her. Thanks for heads up.*

Thomas: *Be firm, but remember how hard this will be for both of them. So also be gentle.*

Me: *I will. x 3.*

My brief text exchange with Thomas has prepared me for what to expect from Mom; I am ready for whatever lies ahead—I tell myself this as I park the rental car in the driveway of the house I grew up in and walk to the front door, kicking up fallen leaves on the sidewalk. *I am ready. I am ready. I am ready.* Except, when I walk in the front door, it is my encounter with Dad that I'm not ready for. Sitting in the family room in his favorite chair, he gives me a quick wave; he is on the phone making a doctor appointment for Mom. I park my carry-on bag in a corner and sit silently on the sofa across from him, listening. He's saying he wants Mom to see a different urologist than she has previously because that doctor never finds anything. The volume on the telephone headset must be set really high, because I can hear the woman on the other end replying that Mom has already seen all of the doctors in their office. Dad says that he himself is a doctor, he has diagnosed that Mom needs a catheter, and he needs her to see a doctor over there who will get this done.

Interrupting his conversation, I speak my first words since arriving: "Dad, tell her you will call her back. You and I need to talk." Barreling right on in with my bossiness a-blazing.

Once he hangs up, I say, "What was that about? Has something new happened?" I'm thinking back to what he'd said in his voicemail a few days ago about some bit of information he has not yet shared.

Dad replies, "No, it's the same issue as before."

And I lose my patience. As quickly as that. "Dad, Mom has run-of-the-mill bladder frequency issues; what you're trying to fix here is the exact opposite. Mom is *not* incontinent. She does *not* need a catheter. And you are *not* her doctor. Mom doesn't need more appointments to fix nonexistent issues. We need to pull out of this spiral. You've called for help almost every day lately about Mom's behavior issues, her dementia, getting worse. We need to face the facts—Mom may no longer be able to stay at home. Which is why I am here. To help sort this out. Let's stay on track."

Dad replies, "You're being mean and you sound just like her. All angry. I can't do anything right. And I can't take this anymore. I'm doing my best, but I can't take care of her."

"I'm sorry, Dad. I didn't mean to be mean. I know you're try-ing to help Mom."

Not a great first two minutes. *Gentle* with Dad, I was not.

Deep breaths. Start over.

Apparently, an hour or so earlier, Mom was quite agitated about my imminent arrival—and quite mad at Dad—but she went back upstairs to bed, even though it's still morning. Dad and I make some coffee and sit at the kitchen table to talk about the realities of putting Mom into a home, without having to worry about her overhearing our conversation and becoming reignited. If Mom does in fact need to be moved to assisted living, we don't have anywhere for her to go—we lost our one opportunity a few days ago when Dad said *no.* Dad mentions a new place he's seen on his walks, not even a mile away. I say *let's go take a look!* And we head out the door, leaving behind our still-hot cups of coffee.

A *much* better next eight minutes.

Because Maplewood Pointe is a brand-new assisted-living fa-cility, there are openings available. Right now. Dad and I take a tour, we talk, and we put a refundable deposit on a studio apart-ment in the memory care section. We decide that if Dad feels the need to hide the deadbolt keys out of fear that Mom will wander out of the house at night, *memory care* is probably where she be-longs, but a nurse will come to the house to do an assessment in a few days, and then we'll know for sure. We don't need to commit to anything today, and I will do some research on this place, but it's possible we could move Mom by the end of next week or so.

We go back to the house for lunch, and while we're making peanut butter sandwiches, Mom comes downstairs. She's much more confused than when I was here in June—she knows who I am but doesn't know the day, month, or year. Her hair isn't clean, and I can wrap my hand completely around her upper arm, even over her pajamas. I snuck this little test in when I was giving her a hug. She doesn't want anything to eat, just roams around a bit—after asking me when I am leaving—and then goes back to bed. While we're eating, I ask Dad about the thing he had left a message about the other day, the thing none of us kids knows about yet, and he says it's that Mom needs a catheter. I don't know if he actually knows what I'm asking about, if he remembers having left that message or why he might have called; I'm pretty sure Dad is just repeating the issue still in his head from this morning. I sigh, in a good way. Relief. I feel a backlog of pressure slowly escaping with my long, drawn-out breath, so relieved the dreaded news isn't a brain tumor, as my brothers and I had feared.

After lunch we go to the grocery store, stopping to share a bit of dessert, a huge chocolate chip cookie, in the cafe before we start shopping. I tell Dad that once we move Mom to Maplewood Pointe (or wherever), we'll have solved only part of the problem, that he will be even more alone, and lonely, than he is now. Whereas, if he were to consider moving to Maplewood Pointe, too, in addition to easily being able to spend time with Mom, he would be in a building full of people he could socialize with, just a block away from restaurants, the library, and other places he could safely walk to. He says he'll think about it, adding that most of his long-time friends in the neighborhood have either moved away or died. Thinking he's referring to the recent death of one of his neighbors, I say, "Yes, it's sad about Mrs. Barnes."

Dad replies, "It's not too sad . . . for years all she did was sit in her house alone."

Along with some rotisserie chicken for dinner, we pick up some gummy bears and Tic Tacs—placebos to replace the bowl of Dramamine for Mom's *vertigo* and the newly added bowl of TUMS for Mom's *nausea,* all of which Dad tried to hide shortly after I arrived this morning. I threw all the medications out and said, *no more.* Mom's ailments are random and imaginary, but if she insists on taking *something,* and he feels like he needs to give her *something,* I want to try replacing that *something* with something that will do no harm.

Shortly before dinnertime, Mom comes downstairs. She says she has vertigo as she walks to the bowl for some Dramamine, but when she sees the mound of gummy bears resting in there she yells, "I have vertigo! I need Dramamine!" *Yells.* Loudly. I have never heard my mom yell except when my brothers and I were kids playing outside in the neighborhood and she needed to call us home for dinner. And that had a very different tone.

I say, "Mom, you don't have vertigo, but those will make you feel better."

Shoving that bowl aside, she replies, "Actually, what I need are TUMS. I'm feeling very nauseated."

I pick up the bowl of Tic Tacs and say, "Try these, Mom. They're even better than TUMS."

She glares at me. *Glares.* (Silently, but still *loudly.*) Mom picks up a pencil lying near the pad of paper by the phone and throws it at Dad, then throws a pen at him; then, screeching (screeeeeching), she pushes Dad in the chest with both hands. Calmly (*gently*), I say, "Mom, it's not okay to throw things or push."

"But he's starving me!"

I get Mom to eat half a banana, only by Not. Giving. Up. Because she's not eaten anything else all day. And then she returns to bed—after asking, again, *when are you leaving?* She's been awake, at most, for about thirty minutes since this morning.

The next day, Thomas and I discuss Mom and Dad's finances; he now has power of attorney for their financial and medical decisions, so he has been able to gather some information. We feel comfortable that they can afford for Mom to live at Maplewood Pointe, at least for a good while, and Dad, too, if he decides to sell their house and move. The cost of the memory care apartment (including meals and Mom's current care needs) is around $5,000 a month at this place, which seems to be in line with other places in the area as far as size, cost, and care package. An assisted-living unit for Dad would cost about $4,000, increasing as care needs increase, pushing their total living expenses toward $10,000 a month, out of pocket. Mom and Dad have a nice nest egg, but it won't last forever—I don't know what we'll do if it runs out. And I wonder what people do, where people go, when they need the sort of care Mom needs but have little to no savings.

With the potentially immediate financial hurdle behind us, I call a moving company and make tentative arrangements for Mom's move next Monday—just over a week away.

Right before the nurse arrives to do Mom's assessment, I steer Dad outside to rake leaves—something he loves to do. Mom has been yelling at him to cancel this appointment since we told her about it, so having him anywhere around when the nurse gets here seems like it might be a problem. And he can release some of his stress—the growing mountain of fears and truths and changes—of which I'm sure he's feeling *a lot*. Mom is absolutely delightful with the nurse, partly, I think, because they're both nurses named Jennie; they bond over that. Eventually, it's determined that memory care is the appropriate setting for Mom, but we don't tell her *that*. We tell her that she's going to be moving to an assisted-living place just down the street. That it's a beautiful place that will be furnished with things from the house, a place where she will be safe and will be served delicious meals and will be able to enjoy performances by local musicians without having to go outside.

Mom says, "It sounds very nice, but I just want to be on the *list*."

I say, in my most perky voice, "Mom, the list is ready, so you get to move over there next week, on Monday!"

She says, "I can go on Thursday."

The next morning, Dad and I go back to look at what will soon be Mom's new home, measuring walls and contemplating what furniture might fit in her one-room apartment and make it feel homey. We also look at an apartment for him—it has a living room and a bedroom, is sunny and bright, and is on the same floor as Mom's apartment. On the *not-locked-in* side of the heavy locked doors. Surprisingly, Dad says he thinks he wants to move, sooner rather than later, that it makes sense for a lot of reasons, but mostly, he wants to be near Mom. His other half, for better or worse, till death do they part. We put down a deposit to hold the apartment for a few days while he thinks things over.

I cancel my return flight home, indefinitely. I will stay until Mom is moved and Dad is settled, one way or another.

Since I've been here, I've kept trying to convince Mom to take a bath, but she keeps saying she'll take one *tomorrow*. Dad says he thinks it's been months since any bathing has occurred, but he hasn't wanted to get involved with that. So last night I told Mom that today would be bath day, and that I would help her, and there would be no excuses accepted.

This morning, when Mom comes downstairs, I remind her that I'm going to help her take a bath in a little bit. She says, "We can do it tomorrow; I have vertigo." And I say, "Actually, we'll do it in about an hour. It will be nice and relaxing, and it will feel good to get all clean and fresh. And your vertigo will have passed by then, so we don't have to worry about that." I've never bathed Mom before, but I did work in nursing homes for years during high school and college, so I have bathed countless other elderly people without a hitch. I can do this.

After (wishfully) giving Mom time to mentally prepare for this thing she has so long avoided, I go into her bedroom, sit next to her—plunking myself on top of the rumpled bedspread and blankets—and chat for a while. Mom lies quietly as I (softly) stroke her arm, talking (softly) about how she used to take care of her patients when she was a practicing nurse—and her own mom, too, after she'd had a stroke. I remind her of how she would help bathe them and how good they would feel when the bath was finished. Taking Mom by the hand, a sweet little lamb, I guide her to the bathroom door, saying, "Okay, lift your arm and I'll help you take off your top."

Suddenly, Mom is no longer a lamb. She is screaming. Wailing. Howling.

Earlier, Dad agreed to stay downstairs during bath time—first, because bathing Mom is the last thing he wants to do at this point in time. And second, because I suggested that since he's unable to say *no* to Mom if she does or doesn't want something, even if it's in her best interest, it might be best if he weren't around. But now, here he is, right in the midst of the mess of things. Mom is clawing at him, screaming. She screams that she has vertigo (dramatically buckling her knees at precisely the point where she screams out *the* word), she screams that she is going to throw up, and she screams that she will take a bath *tomorrow*. Dad is stunned. Bewildered. Panicked. He doesn't know what to do. Or who to help. Since I wasn't expecting the traumatic way things are unfolding, the tub and towel situation is not ready to go, so I ask Dad if he could turn on the warm water, put the plug in the drain, set a towel and washcloth near the tub, and then go back downstairs and try to watch some TV.

Through it all, through all the screaming, I keep talking to Mom, calmly saying, over and over and over, "It's okay. You're going to have a nice bath. It's okay. It will feel so good to be clean. It's okay. Raise your arm, lift your leg." And through it all, through all the screaming, she does as she's asked.

While helping Mom into the tub, I somehow end up in the tub with her, my jeans soaked to the knees as I try to keep her from slipping and try to soothe the wild beast. I start singing "The Wheels on the Bus," and when I forget the words, I just keep starting over at the beginning. Using the handheld showerhead, I run a slow stream of warm water down Mom's back and over her arms. The thrashing and screaming stop. I keep singing. *The wheels on the bus go round and round, round and round, round and round. . . .* And then Mom says how good the water feels, so I move on to shampoo and rinse her hair. The sweet little lamb is back. When Mom is all clean, I get her into some fresh pajamas. I dry her hair, rub lotion on her arms and legs, and trim her nails. Finally, peace and tranquility. But only on the surface; my knees are still shaking. I am mush. I tell Mom we'll do a nice bath like this every couple of days, barely hopeful she will remember only the good parts of this ordeal and actually agree. I already know that when the time comes, if she says *no,* even hints at a *no,* I'm not going any further. I don't have what it takes to go through this again.

In the whirlwind of the past week or so, my brothers and I discussed the possibility of Mom and Dad staying in their house, with a home health aide assisting in caring for Mom instead of moving her somewhere else. We've already moved beyond that idea, but the Bath from Hell underscores why such a setup would never work—the established dynamic between Mom and Dad is so entrenched that an outsider could not possibly succeed in any productive way. With all of my *insider* influence—the history, love, motivation, background information, and new comfort with being bossy—the only thing that kept me from being derailed and running away from the whole disaster was *all of that*. An outsider would have been steamrolled the second Dad went upstairs to help Mom.

I had no idea of the erratic and volatile behaviors that Dad has been dealing with. *No idea.* Neither did Thomas or Jonathan. Dad has been camouflaging the truth for many years—a truth that couldn't be discerned over short visits, phone calls, or even pointed questioning. Honesty and trust were a foundation of our upbringing, so we had no reason to doubt what Dad was telling us—that Mom had vertigo and slept a lot, that he was handling things, that he'd taken care of his family and sick people his whole life, and he would continue to do so (thank you very much, good-bye). Dad was protecting his wife, his life work, his pride, his heart—and he was protecting himself from the truth, from the beginning of the end. So he kept the real truth locked up tight. At those times when my brothers and I tried to dig a little deeper, those times when things didn't seem quite right, we weren't able to really change anything because we weren't able to control anything—until now. Until Dad was finally ready to ask for, and then actually accept, help.

Sadly, it's impossible to make another adult do something, *anything,* if they don't want to do it—a hard lesson I lived and learned in dealing with Joey and his addiction.

Dad must have endured a lot of pain before getting to this point—the point he was trying so hard not to get to. The point where he's too tired to carry on and must hand over the reins—the point where the roles of parent and child completely change. But now, here we are. My brothers and I have been entrusted to take care of the parents who took such good care of us. And we will try mightily to copy their example.

●

The boxes are all packed, full to the brim with Mom's clothes and most treasured belongings, and the movers will be here first thing in the morning. Getting that part ready was easy compared to what's coming next.

Thomas sends me his last text of the day as I'm getting ready for bed: *I'm dreading tomorrow.*

I reply: *Me too.*

We've been plotting for days how to get Mom out of her forever home and into her new apartment with the least amount of trauma. We want to avoid having to literally carry our frail-but-feisty eighty-nine-year-old mom out of the house and into the car and down the road and into Maplewood Pointe and up the elevator and down the hall to her new home—all while she's kicking and screaming. We're not overthinking things; after seeing what I've seen, I know this is a real possibility. So we can't just wing it. We need to be prepared to do whatever's needed to get Mom safely from over here to over there. Josh and I faced a similar conundrum back when we needed to get Joey from India all the way to the United States for the help he needed:

> *Joey was born tenderhearted. When he's around, hugs don't go un-hugged, smiles don't go un-smiled, and upside-down bugs don't go un-uprighted. Yes, Joey is an angel. Except when he's not. Lately unpredictable and explosive, Joey is more likely to slam a clenched fist into the wall and storm from the house than he is to agree with anything or to share a smile. So, if Joey doesn't like the idea of being locked away in a faraway hospital, Josh and I agree there's no way we'll get him there. Shrinking though he may be, Joey is still a sizable young man bursting with stress, testosterone, and whatever else is going on inside him. To get him help, we must first get him on and then off a couple of planes and halfway*

around the world. For us to accomplish this, Joey must be willing to travel. The thought of Josh needing to use his size and strength to contain or restrain Joey on our upcoming journey slips my soul off its axis. So, in the spirit of safe and happy travels, Josh and I agree to lie.

—*The Joey Song,* 3–4

Dad and I have been casually reminding Mom of her upcoming move every day, and she has been casually flinging back the retort that *she is fine, Dad is fine, neither of them is forgetful or unfit, and since they're both medical professionals, they can stay here in the house forever.* Once I started to pack things in boxes, Mom started saying she *isn't going,* but now, as of this morning, she is refusing to speak to—or even look at—me. She is giving me a very cold shoulder. I suspect she'll forget all this soon enough, but it makes me so sad knowing that Mom feels I'm her enemy.

The plan is for Dad to stay with Mom after the movers are finished loading the truck in the morning, and I will follow them over to Maplewood Pointe to get everything into place—clothes put away, bed made, pictures hung, toothbrush by the sink, rosary in her nightstand, and music on—home sweet home, ready for her arrival a short while later. Then I'll go back to the house to get Mom dressed and downstairs while she is still calm; taking Mom down the narrow, curvy staircase later, when she's likely to be agitated, must be avoided. Once she's in position, Thomas will come over to try getting her out of the house. Dad and I plan to skedaddle the second he arrives—since Mom is currently mad at both of us, our presence might spark up some negative energy and doom the whole operation, veering it off into the unknown realms of a nightmare.

I don't think I will sleep tonight. Whatever happens tomorrow, no matter how smoothly it does or doesn't go, it's going to be *short and awful* or *long and awful*. It is going to hurt. All of us. I don't think there's any other way that moving Mom from her forever home can turn out.

The next morning, I text Thomas: *The movers just finished at house, I'm heading to Maplewood Pointe now. Non-eventful with Mom so far.*

Thomas: *Excellent, hopefully she's not saving up. Nervous!*

Me, a few hours later: *Apartment is all set up . . . it looks nice!*

Thomas: *Good job. Now the hard part. I'll leave work in a little while.*

Me, a few minutes later: *Mom just came downstairs on her own, so I quickly blocked the stairs so she can't go back up again—I used two heavy wingback chairs from the living room, so she can't move them. (I told her there are workmen up there.) HURRY if you can!*

Thomas: *Ok, I'll come now.*

Me: *Great! She's going to lay down on living room sofa. She will still be in her PJs, I don't want to get her riled up at this point.*

Getting Mom from the house was much easier than expected; Thomas told her where he was taking her, she took his hand, and now here they are. Dad and I greet Mom, welcoming her to her new home as Thomas opens the apartment door and guides her in. She's happy to see us and comments on how lovely the place is, walking around, touching her stuffed animals, picking up a few family photographs to give them a closer look, recognizing the four-poster bed from my old bedroom and the comfy blue floral chairs from the living room, and wondering how it is that one of her watercolor paintings and some artwork from when the grandchildren were young are hanging on the walls. Everything is going so well. Until Mom announces that she's ready to go home.

"Mom, this is your home now. And Dad will be moving here soon, just down the hall."

She starts screaming. "No, no, nooooo . . . I need to go home! This isn't my home!" Mom is grabbing at Dad, pulling his shirt, his arm, begging, sobbing, wailing, "Help me, help me, help me!"

Thomas swoops Dad out the door and far away before Dad's heart can break any further, and I stay with Mom, trying to help *her* heart understand what's going on. I hover, I hug, I murmur words of comfort that aren't comforting at all, as Mom roams the hallway, up, down, and around, crying, *howling*, pleading with me to take her home. Tears streak her terrified face as she shakes and pounds the locked doors separating her from everything she knows in the world. No matter what I say, the only thing Mom understands is that she is *not* home and *not* with Dad.

I ask a nursing assistant to stay with Mom for a while, help-ing settle her into her new surroundings once I leave. After giving Mom a long hug and telling her that Dad and I will return tomor-row, I quietly slip out of the apartment and into the hallway while Mom's attention is focused on trying to convince the aide to call Dad or a taxi so she can go home. Fighting back tears, trying to hold them in until I get out to my car, I'm halfway down the hall when I hear Mom calling my name. *Sandy . . . stop! Wait! Please! I need to go home! Take me home.* Turning, I see her chasing me, try-ing to catch up to me, arms out, stumbling along in pink pajamas and sheepskin slippers, crying and afraid. The aide moves in to redirect Mom's attention, and I try to enter the code into the key-pad near the locked doors to complete my escape, barely able to see the numbers through the tears I'm no longer able to contain.

I know Mom is where she needs to be. She will be safe and cared for by people who know what they're doing. But even so, *this hurts*. My heart aches as I think of Mom, all alone tonight, scared and unable to understand what's happening—or why the people who love her let it happen. I feel sort of like I did when leaving Joey and Rick on their first day of kindergarten.

Or when leaving Joey in a hospital for treatment:

Nobody eats the hearty breakfast served outside on the terrace under the warm December sky that nobody notices. We just move the sausages and eggs around on our plates until it's time to depart for Joey's appointment. The three of us trudge across the street to the sprawling hospital, but only two of us know what's coming. (I'm only trudging on the outside; on the inside I'm running away.) The closer we get—to the glass doors at the main entrance, to the sign aiming us to the psychiatric ward on the sixth floor, to the metal door behind which he'll be locked up—the more halting Joey's steps become. And the harder it becomes to keep my trembling knees from folding. I watch as my son's grudging trust turns to rabid anger at the realization that he's been duped. A whirling dervish of elbows and legs, Joey turns on me, face twisted and pleading. As he's taken away by the white-coated staff trying to restrain him, I claw at the air between us, crying, begging Joey to understand what is to him an inexplicable betrayal.

—*The Joey Song,* 9

Doing what's right isn't easy.

Over the years, I've heard plenty of people say they could never put their parents into a home, that they love their parents too much to ever do that. (I can remember a time when those words came out of my own mouth, too.) I've also heard variations of this sentiment—and seen how judgmental (and blinding) preformed ideas can be—while sitting in addiction support groups:

Josh and I are the veterans in this circle. The jaded parents, the beaten parents, the parents Letting Go, while the others are still Hanging On. The others, the still hopeful—the parents who look and sound like we did not long ago—to them our Letting Go doesn't look a whole lot like love. They haven't yet been dragged through the dark places we've been dragged through. They haven't yet been pummeled into submission. No, they haven't yet been whittled down to the point of understanding that Letting Go is love. . . .

Following some discussion, someone coughs up the fur ball stuck in the collective-other parents' throats.

"I can't do what Josh and Sandy are prepared to do. I'm not as strong . . . I want him to know he is loved."

—The Joey Song, 183

Experience. My list of things to Never Judge keeps growing longer. And I've learned to at least *try* hearing with my ears and eyes rather than with my preconceived notions.

I take Dad out for dinner, trying to make this day a little bit better even though I know I can't. When we get back to the house, he is unsettled, jumping from his chair in the family room to do something for Mom at every old-house creak and groan. Until he remembers, again, that she is not here. Dad has been slowly losing Mom to dementia for years—but tonight he faces another, different, loss. Tonight, he's missing the physical presence of the person he loves more than anyone in the whole world, too.

The focus now shifts to getting Dad moved to the same place as Mom in just two weeks' time, in addition to getting the house on the market and arranging to sell all of Mom and Dad's stuff. But, weary from the toll of ripping Mom out of her old home and plunking her into her new one, I'm off to a slow start the next morning. I've been reading the newspaper and am well into my second cup of coffee before I change out of my pajamas and set up my laptop on the kitchen table, finally ready to research the next steps. I can see Dad out the back window, dressed in khakis and his favorite plaid shirt, bagging up leaves. He's really in superior physical form, has hauled almost a dozen bags to the curb so far (and it's not even ten), and is living his motto: *I can keep moving because I keep moving.* And today, after the epic horribleness of yesterday, Dad definitely needs to be moving. I don't know what he's going to do once he no longer has his yard to work in.

Before I can give this more thought, in pops a text from Josh: *Hi, hope all is well! Let me know when you are free to talk. I need to go over alimony payments for this year and beyond.*

Four years after our divorce, Josh wants to reduce my alimony by more than half and is proceeding with his intent, effective immediately. He doesn't ask how I'm going to now afford life; he has started over, launching a new career under the wings of a couple of his husband's businesses and so, apparently, can barely afford me. This makes no sense—Josh's recent beach house reunion and other travels have given the impression of the exact *opposite* of financial constriction.

The only thing that makes sense is that we've now become a cliché.

But I don't have the capacity to give this any more thought; 100 percent of my focus is needed here, so I'll wait until I get back home, whenever that is, to let my hurt, fear, and confusion loose. Even as each and every day, starting today, I'll be nibbling away at my old-age nest egg and moving closer to realizing my fear of one day eating cat food and being homeless. For now, I wrap it all up in the crusty old callous I've developed over the years, protecting myself from what I can do nothing about right now (if ever). I'm so tired of Josh ripping the rug out from under my life. Over and over and over. I'm so tired of *life*. I'm just so tired.

I reply: *I'm at my mom and dad's. Things are very busy here. Nothing has changed since the last time you tried to reduce your alimony commitment. I still require the agreed upon income to live on; I planned my future on it. So, if you wish to pursue this please contact your divorce attorney.*

Dad has disappeared from my view out the window, so I go outside to see what he's up to—at least that's what I pretend. Really, I just want to be near someone who loves me. He's near the open garage doors, blowing leaves outward into a pile, but he stops when he sees me. Smiling. We talk about all the bags of leaves he has collected and what he might like for lunch later—avoiding the sad topic of Mom for the moment. We're both still just trying to stay afloat. And then, after I notice the blackened wall around the outlet he's plugged into, we talk about the dangers of using a light-duty indoor extension cord for heavy-duty outdoor equipment. Another minute or two, and we might have had a fire.

Over lunch, peanut butter sandwiches again (Dad's favorite), we talk about the furnishings he might like to take to his new apartment. From a two-story house full of treasured items collected over decades with Mom, he's going to have to choose a mere handful of things. The apartment he's moving into is *tiny*; the whole thing—a bedroom, living room, and bathroom—is about equal in size to his modestly proportioned, early-1960s-style family room. There will be room for a twin bed, an upright dresser with bookshelves, and a small computer table in the bedroom, and in the living room there will be room for a sofa, a coffee table, his favorite recliner, the narrow roll-top desk from his den, and a TV. On one end of the living room there is a kitchenette with a sink, mini fridge, and microwave, so there's also a counter on which he can put a few things.

Thinking about the layers and layers of loss—how Dad's whole world and life's history are so drastically shrinking—my next bite of sandwich is difficult to swallow. I try to distract from the sadness I feel hanging over the table by talking about the details of decorating: *How about this painting? That lamp?* Dad is, I think, overwhelmed. He tells me to choose whatever I think will fit and look good, that he'd like to focus on getting the yard work done before he moves out. He'd like the outside to look its best for potential buyers—adding that he will be close enough to walk over and mow and check on things every now and then until the house sells. There's no need for me to pop that bubble; it's eventually going to pop itself.

So most days I'm inside packing and sorting, and Dad is outside cleaning the garage or the birdbaths, getting ready for the unimaginable events that are really going to happen—and soon. We also sprinkle some fun into each day—like going to the arboretum (Dad's favorite place) or to lunch at his favorite restaurant.

And we visit Mom.

Slowly, she's adjusting, and on some days things are better than others. Yesterday when we arrived, Mom was sitting in her chair, dressed in real clothes, her alarm clock and glasses in hand, all ready to go in case the police came to save her (she said she had given the house address to the nurse so the police would know where she belongs). But Dad and I could be the ones to take her home, instead. RIGHT NOW!

Mom turns into the scary stranger I gave a bath to whenever Dad and I prepare to leave her, making departures dreadful for everyone. The nurse has suggested we not use the word *home* except when saying things like *what a lovely home you have.* So we no longer say *it's time for us to go home, we love you, goodbye.* Instead, we ease our way out, with Dad leaving first, saying something like *I need to check your mailbox,* and I leave a few minutes later saying something like *I have a meeting with the nurse.* We've also learned to get our hugs in when we arrive because hugging Mom at the end makes our imminent departure too obvious, instantly firing up the emotions and trauma we're trying to avoid. It's all very deceptive, which makes Dad and me feel crummy, but it's less crummy than what happens if we're not a couple of sneaks.

Once, after a smooth early exit, Dad had to return to Mom's room because he forgot the code to get out the locked door at the end of her wing. He asked me to remind him but couldn't hear my reply so I kept repeating the code more and more loudly—until Mom finally yelled the numbers out to him (then asked what the numbers were for). Now we've got the code written down on a piece of paper in his wallet.

We have been practicing for Dad to visit with Mom on his own—once he lives here, he's going to have to extricate himself from her apartment several times every day until things with her settle down. He knows what to do to limit the trauma and drama, but he hasn't done it alone and needs some confidence; I don't want Dad to avoid seeing Mom out of fear of a devastating departure. The first time we tried this, I stayed downstairs in the lobby, sitting on the little sofa and picking up a newspaper from an end table, thinking I might be parked there for quite a while. But five minutes later, Dad popped out of the elevator . . . with Mom on his arm. Seeing the front doors, she bolted straight for the sunshine and freedom with a screech. Leaping to my feet, I grabbed my sweet little mama-turned-howling-tornado and somehow got her back on the elevator and back behind the locked doors where she belongs—on my own. Dad was frozen in place by the icy words I had just snapped at him, so no help there, and assisted-living places don't have orderlies. I was weak in the knees for hours.

The first night we ate dinner with Mom, she got up from the table where we were seated and began to march purposefully around the dining room, adjusting wheelchairs and tucking in napkins, taking care of the other residents as she would have taken care of her patients back in her nursing days. One woman stood in the middle of the room and wouldn't move when Mom tried to help get her seated. When Mom came back to our table, she whispered that the woman belongs in a place for people with dementia. So Mom has no understanding of where she is, which is good.

Mom and Dad's house isn't officially on the market until after Dad moves out, but the Realtor has already lined up the first showing, so Dad and I have been cleaning house like crazy. The dust we stirred up somehow set off the fire alarm, and since Dad couldn't remember the code, we soon had firemen, police, and a bunch of neighbors swarming the place—which turned out to be how Dad announced to the neighborhood that his house is up for sale and he will be moving in just a few days.

I wasn't sure this day would actually happen, even though I've been canceling utilities, changing mailing addresses, and transferring medical records—and we've been negotiating over a buyer's offer on the house. More than once, Dad has declared that he wanted to stop everything and bring Mom back home. But here we are, one month to the day since my arrival, opening the door to Dad's new apartment, all cozy and homey, to spend some time looking around, showing him where all of his things are tucked away, and getting him settled in.

Dad has been nervous about eating dinner in the assisted-living dining room—*where will I sit? Who will I sit with?* An insecurity at any age. So I eat with him that first night, finding us a table with two other men and getting the conversation moving over a meal of beef stroganoff and salad. When I leave, Dad and his new friends are talking about a concert down the hall tomorrow afternoon, and Dad says he's looking forward to going.

Everyone is where they need to be, safe and, hopefully, soon to be happy. For the first time in weeks, I can breathe.

My plan is to stay in Minnesota for another week, getting things ready for the estate sale, which will happen after I leave, squeezed into the calendar of a local company, under Thomas's watch. And I want to make sure Dad is settling in okay and that Mom's settling-in is getting better. Mom doesn't understand that Dad is now living just down the hall, even though we have taken her to see his apartment. So every time he visits her, she gets upset, wanting him to take her *home.* Now! Our practice drills didn't help much. But Jonathan came from California for a couple of days to help Mom and Dad with the process of adapting to their new life—and to see the house in Golden Valley, where we grew up, one last time.

Mom and Dad have so many unique and beautiful antiques and works of art. I remember when my brothers and I were growing up, they would say things like *someday we will pass this on to you.* That was a nice plan, but the reality is our homes are smaller and were long ago fully furnished, none of the grand-children are in a position to acquire such things (even if they wanted them), and no one can afford to ship furniture across the country or to put things in storage for years on end. And because there are countless other aging parents in the same position as Mom and Dad, the market is saturated, which means everything they own will be sold for far less than it's worth, and whatever doesn't sell will be given away. I wish this weren't true. But the sale of the remains of Josh's and my life together—including things such as fine antiques and crystal—is just one of a million such examples.

Bracing myself for the job ahead, I take a moment to inhale deeply. Then, slowly, slowly, I exhale, a long breath that unexpectedly ends with a quiver. I begin my hunt through their house, looking for the stuff of *them*. The stuff of Mom and Dad. The things that shouldn't be rummaged through at a rummage sale no matter what. The family photographs, the cardboard box full of our when-we-were-little-kids artwork, and the drawer full of cards made by the grandkids over the years. The blue wool cap Dad wore in the Navy, and the white linen nursing cap Mom received when she became a registered nurse. The pocket watch that belonged to Dad's dad, and the yellow-with-filigree pin that belonged to Mom's mom. Dad's hand-carved and hand-painted folksy Swedish figurines and some of his old tools. Mom's cookbooks and Grandma's rosette iron. I look through every room—every drawer, every closet, every nook and cranny—trying not to see or feel or think too much, but I fail. As with the times I've had to do this same thing with *the stuff of Joey*, the pieces of Mom and Dad's life are piling up in my heart, one on top of the other, and the weight of it all crumples my knees:

> *There was a time, back when all this started, when I'd wanted to go through Joey's things; I'd wanted to see what I would discover, uncover, about Joey and his life, but I hadn't the stomach for it then. I still don't have the stomach, I no longer have the desire, and, somehow, I've acquired the wisdom not to go sticking my heart in with piranhas. So I lug Joey's boxes to the street without even looking at the potent relics inside. But I know what's here. I know the significance of the college folders, all neatly labeled but empty. A blue-and-yellow ski jacket with crinkled lift tickets on the zipper. Board shorts and board. Fishing poles and fishing magazines. Towels from his dorm and a blender from his first*

apartment. Swiping at the tears rolling down my dusty face,
I Let Go. Some more.

—*The Joey Song,* 192–93

I make one last visit to see Mom and Dad the night before heading back to Texas. Dad wonders if I've ever seen his apartment; that has me worried. I remind him that I helped him to move in last week. He talks about how he is going to miss mowing his yard and sleeping in his old bedroom, but he says the move is a good thing, for both him and Mom, even if it will take some time to adjust. I tell Dad I will be back in a few months, giving us both something to look forward to and to hang on to, and I'm not the only one getting emotional when we say our goodbyes.

Mom is up, dressed in real clothes, and sitting in her comfy chair working on a crossword puzzle when I walk in to her apartment. She smiles when she sees me, ear to ear, and seems to assume I'm visiting from Texas. She has no memory of me at their house or the whole ugly move just three weeks ago (thank goodness). She tells me about the delicious food here, how beautiful everything is—furnished with stuff just like furniture they had in their house!—and how nice the staff are. She says she would recommend the place to anybody, and for the first time, she doesn't mention going home. My brothers and I have been worried Mom's adjustment might take months, but it seems this new world has already, and quite suddenly, displaced her old world. Sad (oh, so sad), but good.

Then Mom lowers her voice, leaning in as if to confide something ominous, saying, "I have something to tell you." I lean forward in my chair, too, instantly alarmed. My brothers and I trust the people here to take good care of Mom and Dad, but, sadly, we can't know if this is always true. She starts by announcing that

Dad is selling their house, and then says, "He has abandoned me." I say, "Mom, no! Dad hasn't abandoned you! He lives here now, too, in an apartment on this same floor, very close by. Dad loves you more than anything in the whole world—please find peace in that—and he would never abandon you, *I promise*." Then she says how cute my shoes are and is off, thankfully, in another direction.

Tomorrow morning I will head back home, one and a half months after flying here for just a couple of days, never imagining that everything—every last thing—would so rapidly be turned upside down and inside out. And so tonight, as I spend my last night in my childhood home, I'm feeling sort of stunned. And weepy. And alone. I'm sad for Mom and Dad, for all the scary changes they've endured—oh, how I wish they could have stayed in their home all the way to the end, their clocks quietly winding down in the comfort of *here*. And I'm sad for me—the loss of some more supposedly rock-solid pieces of life is just beginning to sink in.

One last time, I walk through the rooms of my past. The house is so quiet—until the silence becomes filled with the voices, the laughter, and the love that lived here for fifty years.

I remember, I see, I feel so much.

I remember eagerly pulling Josh through the front door to meet Mom and Dad for the first time—my future and past coming together—and I see the two of us, hand in hand, cutting our wedding cake in front of the living-room window. I feel the happiness of Rick and Joey as they painted pictures with Mom at the dining-room table and carved wooden ducks and dogs with Dad on the deck, and the fun Jonathan, Thomas, and I had as we lay on the floor playing board games or building with Legos. Moving to the stairway, I climb halfway up before turning to sit, right at the bend—the exact center of our home. The main artery, connecting everyone to all the comings and goings and goings-on. Looking up, I see a couple of petrified spitballs still clinging to the high ceiling—the handiwork of one or the other of my brothers—and I remember one or the other finding himself in some trouble because of that. I remember stomping up the stairs when I was *sent to my room* and gliding down the stairs in my shiny blue prom dress when I was a long-ago sweet sixteen. In my mind, I can smell the aroma of molasses cookies wafting up and around, all the way from the kitchen to my second-floor bedroom, and I can feel the snug feeling of sitting in the kitchen with Mom and a big glass of milk as we munched on some of her fresh-baked cookies and talked.

Even in my sleep, tonight, I remember, I see, I feel so much.

As the sun rises, I lock the front door and wheel my small suitcase down the sidewalk, stopping for a moment to touch the trunk of the towering maple tree in the front yard, one of three trees that Dad planted long ago in the name of my two brothers and me, giving us permanent roots in this place, even though this place, for us, is no more. Turning, I take one last look at the most beautiful yellow house with black shutters, ever.

Goodbye, house.

I'm so tired. So tired of living with heartache and wishes. The heartache of so much loss. And the wishes for things, *so many things,* to be different. Wishing for the things that were meant to *still be.* Wishing for things to stop ending.

6

The Golden Valley

Happiness is a form of courage.

—GEORGE HOLBROOK JACKSON

THE FLOODGATES HAVE OPENED. My tears and my sadness flow forth unrestrained. A deluge. A release. All the feelings I've been holding in for six weeks (rolled up with all the feelings I've been holding in for months and years) are coming out, riding on waves of sheer exhaustion. The unrelenting need to try making sense of what makes no sense at all—in so many ways, with so many people—has worn me to a nub. Sprawled on my stomach across my bed, I ache for a comforting hand on my shoulder, or to be wrapped in the arms of someone who feels what I feel, who cares what I feel, and whose love would absorb some of the pain. My aloneness adds to the sadness already filling me up to the brim. A spontaneous cleansing, this happens every once in a while—my body, brain, and heart team up to say it's time to shed some of the *sad* to make room for some *happy*. For a tomorrow, a soul, filled with more strength than tears. And so, I don't hold back.

Back home now from my roots in Golden Valley, I'm grieving the loss of the house I grew up in, the loss of my parents as *parents,* and the loss of their *golden years* dream. I'm grieving the loss of yet another belief in the man I once thought I knew—the essence of the man to whom I was married—and the ongoing loss of my son to The Addict who consumes him. I'm grieving the loss of my family—both families: the one I was born into and the one I made—and the loss of life's most important and everlasting connections, which have been lost with these losses. And I'm grieving the loss of my sense of security and of life as I knew it (again), and so the loss of a whole bunch more dreams, too.

So, in crying, I'm working through quite a backlog of material. *Unrealized dreams.* This cry will take some time.

> *Dreams. So lofty and pie in the sky. Like clouds. Yet solid enough to hang your hat on. So, for something that never actually happened,* unrealized *dreams are a heavy load. Like a dowager's hump, the weight has me emotionally stooped. The pain is crippling.*

> *My dreams—for my children, for my family, for me—had no boundary. Some dreams were big and lofty, like happiness and personal successes, while other dreams were more low-key, like for everyone to be all snug-as-a-bug. I dreamed of togetherness at family trips, holidays, days at the beach, or celebrating life's great events—or being together for life's not-so-great events, too. Some dreams were as simple as chatty phone calls, sharing jokes, or checking in on what's up. My dreams had no boundary, and so there's no boundary to my agony now that those dreams are gone.*

> *I mourn the dreams that aren't to be. I mourn the dreams that should have been, the dreams that could have been, and even the silly little daydreams and long-shot pipe dreams. Carried away, like a towering tree in a storm, things that once seemed solid, secure, and certain are gone.*

> *Where do dreams go when they die?*

> —*Tending Dandelions*, 123

A few nights later, all dried up and dried off—my composure put back together and my feelings put back in the place where I store them—I reach out to some friends, ready now for the comfort of their presence, love, and support. Tonight there's a supermoon, a full moon that is bigger and brighter than usual, so we gather around the firepit in my neighbor's backyard, talking about life and hurt and healing, and we watch as the moon slowly rises and shines in the darkness—as does my spirit. There's great power in friendships.

Gazing up at the moon, I suddenly feel the quiet presence of Joey—I feel he is close even though he is far away, and I haven't seen or heard from him in over a year. I bask in this feeling, believing he might be feeling the same connection, gazing up at this same moon, too.

You, my child, are far, far, away—I think you'd be far, far away even if you lived nearby.

We no longer share the same house or same dreams, holidays, or interests. We rarely even share a pleasant conversation. But that doesn't mean we're not connected. Whether you feel it or not, I'm with you every moment of every day. And wherever you are, we will always share the same moon.

When I miss you (which is always), and when I ache for some time with the son that addiction has stolen away, I step outside and sit down in the quiet night air, waiting for the moon to rise. I look up at this thing that is so far, far away—just like you are to me (and I am to you). But I know that you, too, can see it. Touch it with your eyes. And I feel your presence.

Tonight I will look up at the moon—the same moon hanging in the sky above you—and I will find peace in that

connection. Maybe you will be looking up at the same time,
at the same moon, too.

—Tending Dandelions, 186

With the weather still summerlike here in Texas, I spend some
time working in the backyard, my haven, wanting things to look
nice when Rick arrives for Thanksgiving. I fill the bird feeders
with seed for my little bird friends, and, chuckling to myself, I
follow the muddy-but-cute armadillo footprints tracked across
my patio into the garden beds, trying to discover where the little
critters are sneaking in under the fence—they like to dig around
in the dirt, uprooting my flowers with their snouts, so I'd like to
block their entrance and keep them out.

This year, Rick and I join my friend Cindy and her family
for Thanksgiving dinner. The whole big clan. We haven't established our own tradition, not since our own family fell apart—
Thanksgiving isn't a holiday meant for just two people; it needs
a crowd and a hubbub of activity and lots of dishes full of side
dishes—but each year we've tried something new, and each year
has been lovely in its own unique way. Early in the day, I get a turkey roasting in the oven and bake some apple-sage stuffing and an
upside-down apple-pecan pie, filling the house with the aromas of
the holiday, before Rick and I and a small cadre of helpers carry our
contributions across the street to add to the epic feast: a smorgas-
bord of deliciousness, it includes both a smoked and a deep-fried
turkey, too, to round out our turkey trifecta. Cindy's crew is lively
and warmhearted, and Rick knows most of them from living in
India and from previous visits, so this Thanksgiving is about as
close to *being with family* as being without family can be.

I've been waiting until the end of Rick's visit to tell him about
Josh's plan to cut back on my alimony, not wanting to ruin his

whole time here and having previously decided it was better to tell him in person rather than over the phone, back when the news was new. After much inner debate on how much I should share with (or burden) my younger son, my belief that he needs to know the truth won. We can't be a real family (of two) with only one of us knowing what is going on. My future has been shaken. *I* am shaken. And whatever affects my financial well-being will affect him, too, including my ability to travel to see him (to actually *be* a family) and my ability to take care of myself—financially and otherwise—till the end of time (which, given my parents' physical—if not mental—health, may be another forty years). Secrets, and the inevitable revealing of unwelcome surprises, are, as I've learned, poison.

Over coffee this morning, we sit at the kitchen table talking about his dad, and then Joey, which stirs up the sadness of what life has become. My sweet, solid, grown-up son cries for the first time (that I've seen) since he was a young child. Before Rick slowly walks to his room, yet another *his room* in yet another house he is not attached to, I give him a hug—the I-don't-want-to-let-go kind of hug—and tell him how sorry I am that our family, his family, is so broken. But there isn't a word for this kind of sorry.

Since returning from Golden Valley, I've been getting my old-age ducks in a row—well, in a more orderly row than I already had them. I've been making sure the state of my affairs is clear and official so Rick won't run into the problems we ran into with Mom and Dad (who *thought* they had their old-age ducks in a row). The trauma of it all has Thomas doing the same thing for the sake of his kids, too. When something happens to me, Rick is the one who will be handling things, so my health care directive, power of attorney, will, and financial information can't be hard to find, mysterious, halfway done, or of the you-know-what-I-want variety. And, as uncomfortable as it is, Rick needs to know what's up and where things are; it would be stupid to avoid a conversation about a situation that requires a conversation—a conversation that can't be avoided forever—one way, or with one person, or another.

So, after Rick spends some time alone recovering from the difficult conversation earlier, I squeeze in one more difficult conversation—which actually isn't difficult at all, just matter-of-fact—before his departure tomorrow. And I give him a letter to hold on to in case, years down the road, he needs to use it:

Dear Future Self,

If you're reading this letter, it's probably because Rick is showing you the copy you gave him many years ago—either because you forgot where your copy is (or that you even wrote this), you don't remember your desire to move gracefully on to the next stage of life, or you don't recognize or acknowledge that that time is here.

I've just returned home after spending six weeks with Mom and Dad, moving them into memory care and assisted living and getting their house ready to sell. I had to separate them from the home they built and lived in together for 55 years, and from each other after 60 years of marriage. Sadly, dementia had invaded their minds and lives, and I had to invade every corner of their home and personal space and privacy, while figuring out how to navigate treating them like parents and children at the same time. Nobody was prepared for this, so it was more traumatic than it needed to be, for everyone.

If you're reading this letter, Future Self, it's because you learned from experience, and you want Rick to intervene when it becomes apparent to him that you need supervised living (even if it's not apparent to you).

So, if Rick has pulled out this letter, listen, trust, believe.
Today, and in the days and months ahead.

Sandy
(Your younger, not-yet-senile self)

Later, I send a text to Thomas: *After seeing a movie with Rick this afternoon, a theater we've been to before, I got all confused with east and west and went the wrong direction instead of driving toward home. Rick said, "This is the first sign, Mom."*

Thomas: *I had my first sign so long ago I forgot when it was.*
Me: *Haha . . . me too, but Rick doesn't know that . . . !*

•

Over the past months, Mom and Dad have adjusted to their new home—their *old* home is just a pleasant memory now. But it's been a pretty rocky adjustment at times. Like when Mom and Dad were plotting to move back to their house that was not quite officially sold, even if it was empty of furniture and there was no way to keep Mom safe.

They were simply being pulled like the tide to the moon, to the place, to the life that was theirs, in the rhythm of *forever*. Until, eventually, they simply *forgot*.

The seasons have changed from fall to winter to spring. Hope blooms that Mom and Dad are truly settled. I'm sitting at my desk, placed so that the view from my chair is of the garden out my front window. I watch the bees bob from flower to flower while I chat on the phone with some of the wonderful women I've come to know over the years—the warrior moms making a difference in the world of addiction, each in their own way. We're working on an itinerary for a speaking tour I'll be doing on the East Coast in the fall, trying to string together the invitations in a way that will keep my drive in more of a straight line than a doodle. It's been a very productive morning. I'm not prepared for the next call I answer—the nurse from Maplewood Pointe is recommending that Mom be placed on hospice, a philosophy of care focused on *quality of life* during the time she has left, which is likely no more than six months. I'm stunned. I had no idea this was coming. Physically, Mom has seemed—all along, relatively speaking—fine.

I want to hear Mom's voice. And I want to tell her I love her. But she won't talk on the phone, so I ask Dad to tell her for me. Then I say that all of us will be there soon, all the far-flung kids and grandkids, all at the same time—not adding what Dad may or may not understand: for one last time.

After coordinating travel plans with my brothers and Rick, I send a message through the grapevine to Joey; I want to give him the chance to see Grandma one last time. I want him to say his goodbyes along with the rest of us, if he wants to. I add, "But if you can't make it, don't worry. Grandma knows how much you love her. I talk about you all the time." So Joey now knows he's always a part of our life and love, and he has these words to hold on to, no matter what.

When Joey replies, he is sad about the circumstances but excited to see everyone in just a few days. So now I'm both ecstatic and nervous. I *can't wait* to hug my sweet son, but I don't know what to expect—I hope for the best, but it has been two long years since we've had any contact. I dust off my boundary lines, the ones I haven't needed to use in a while, and remind Joey that his quick one-night trip north must be peaceful and all about Grandma, while silently reminding myself that I'm in control of my own behavior *only*, which includes tightening boundaries up really tight, if I must.

Mom is in bed when Joey, Rick, and I arrive at her apartment, followed by Thomas and his kids and Jonathan and his family. Surely our last time all together before her time comes to an end— but Mom doesn't know this, of course. For two days, we drift in and out for short visits, in varying groups, not wanting to overwhelm her. Mom has a wheelchair now but won't use it; unaware of her deteriorating condition, she happily teeters her way from her bed to sit in a comfy chair once in a while, waving off help. And when she's ready for us to leave, she says, "You must be tired, go take a nap." Or "You must be hungry, go eat some lunch." I notice the Hummel figurine on her nightstand, a baby Jesus lying in the manger—something Mom has always loved, so when she moved here it became more than just a holiday decoration. Mom has covered it in toilet paper, like a blanket, up to the chin and tucked in at the edges. No matter what, always a mommy.

This time spent with Mom, the whole family together, is exquisitely painful and achingly beautiful. As is this time together with my two sons. The roots of love are deep, curling like ribbons around hearts and minds—a gift, unseen, but forever.

●

"I am a doctor; she is my wife."

Dad's two main roles—taking care of Mom and being a doctor—have gotten all jumbled up. He continues to try taking care of Mom as the practicing physician he once was—unaware of his cognitive limitations and with the best of intentions—and keeps raising a ruckus with the Maplewood Pointe staff, over and over and over, putting himself at risk of having to be moved somewhere else. He has been smuggling Mom a prescription drug that he gets from another resident, something to treat her nonexistent vertigo since he forgot about Dramamine. He has been buying hemorrhoid cream for Mom's *headaches* (at her demand), which she slathers all over her forehead, gooping up her hair. And he gets angry when the hospice nurses give Mom medication for pain.

"Morphine is addicting. There's nothing your mom needs that TUMS can't fix." TUMS, which he keeps well stocked in a paper cup in Mom's nightstand drawer.

I've had endless conference calls with Dad and the nurse, resulting in nothing more than a swirl of endless loops. Dad agrees to stop medicating Mom, and Maplewood Pointe sets up ways to monitor Dad's interactions with Mom, but he somehow sneaks into her apartment unseen or hides medications in his pockets (in Ziploc bags) to avoid detection by the aides. This is all so out of character for a man who has followed every rule all his life—but they can't keep Dad if he keeps breaking the rules now.

Dad is hurting Mom with his help—and he would die if he knew that. Right now, I'm feeling about him like I've so often felt about Joey: I just want to get in his brain and shuffle things around to make him think and do the things he needs to think and do to make things okay. It must be very hard to be him, not understanding what's happening but thinking he does and always getting into trouble.

A few days after my trip to Minnesota with the whole family, the nurse at Maplewood Pointe calls to say Mom has been having abdominal pain all morning; she is moaning and in real discomfort but doesn't want to go to the doctor because she has *vertigo*, and Dad agrees with Mom. I say, "Mom doesn't get a say in this, and neither does Dad. They are unable to make decisions about their health. Getting her to a doctor will be a nightmare if she doesn't want to go, so call an ambulance. And don't let Dad go with her—he will just confuse things, using his ingrained doctor persona, telling everyone what he thinks is happening. I will call Thomas to see if he can get over there as quickly as possible."

Dad carries himself in a very professional manner; he is well put together and well spoken, and it takes a while to recognize his reliance on repetition, or that his words aren't always reliable. All of this can be dangerous for Mom. A hard truth, but a truth. She must be protected.

After the ambulance takes Mom away, solo, Dad calls me, livid. "I know you think I'm mentally decrepit, but there's nothing wrong with her. I'm going to take a taxi to the hospital and give them her history." After yelling a few more things at me, he hangs up, hard.

It's midafternoon when I get an update from Thomas. For the past hour, I've been chopping vegetables from the fridge, something to keep myself busy while leaving my mind free to worry, so I set that project aside and go sit on the living-room sofa. He texted this morning to let me know he arrived at the hospital not long after Mom did, and that Dad was already there, but he hasn't had a chance to text back with more news until now. *Dad gave Mom some sort of medicine last night. He's been quite defiant, saying he's capable of being her doctor, but when I asked him what he gave her, he couldn't remember. Maybe Xanax. Who knows where he got whatever it was. They're keeping Mom overnight. She keeps saying she wants to reschedule and doesn't understand she's in the hospital.*

Before I can reply, Dad calls. Thomas had just returned him to his apartment. Once I hang up, I text Thomas back. *Dad just called. He had zero recall of his heated call this morning, didn't remember we had even talked at all. His current recollection of events is that Mom was in discomfort, he brought in a friend, the two of them decided she needed to get to the hospital so they called an ambulance and he went with her to the hospital. He was SO mad at me this morning. Yelling at me. I really hate that we're having these sorts of moments during his waning years. But I guess there's comfort in realizing he doesn't remember. I wish I could forget though.*

The next morning, Thomas texts with an update: *The hospital called to tell me Mom was being discharged, but then Dad called to say he canceled the discharge to have her "urinary retention" reviewed. I just talked to the hospital again, she's being discharged—with a catheter—and has follow-up appointments Monday.*

Me: *What? She doesn't need a catheter. She's not incontinent, she knows when she has to go, she doesn't have accidents. This is crazy. I can't believe they listened to Dad on this. He is very confused and is confusing everyone else.*

This is horrifying. Absolutely horrifying. And yet, in a way, it is beautiful. Even though Dad's mind isn't always clear, the love in his heart is—and with every beat, it compels him to keep taking care of his bride of sixty years.

A few days later, on Monday morning, Dad calls while I'm outside filling the birdbath. I've been keeping my phone close, and as I pull it from my pocket, I feel the dread I've been dreading. We talk for only a few seconds; then I make a quick phone call to Maplewood Pointe and send Thomas a quick text. *Dad just called to tell me that Mom doesn't want to go to her doctor appointment so he is going to remove her catheter himself! I said NO! But he said YES and hung up. I called the nurse and she is headed up to intervene.*

Me: *Update: The nurse told Dad he may NOT take out Mom's catheter, and since Mom is refusing to go to the doctor, they've called an ambulance to take her to the ER to have it removed. They think this is the best and only option. Also, they're keeping an eye on Dad; the nurse thinks he might still try to remove the catheter himself before the ambulance gets there.*

Thomas: *I called Dad, told him this has to stop, that I know he's trying to take care of Mom but he's going to get himself kicked out of Maplewood Pointe and I don't want that to happen because I care about him.*

Me: *I'm glad you told him you care about him. I told him that, too, but in an angry tone of voice—I'd already lost my patience by then and couldn't soften it up.*

So now, everyone—me, Thomas, Jonathan, the nurse—keeps repeating this mantra to Dad, hoping it sticks: "You need to be Mom's companion; being her doctor is not your job. Just be her friend and enjoy your time together. If you think something's not right, steer your concern to the staff; don't try to solve her health issues yourself." But if Dad can't do this, if he continues to treat Mom as a patient while using questionable remedies and procedures, what do we do? We might have to consider moving Dad and Mom apart—but that might very well kill them both. The only other option is to leave them here together—but then, well, whatever happens, happens.

From what I've seen of Alzheimer disease, up close and in the trenches, the reality my family is living is nothing like how it should be—at least compared to how it's portrayed in the commercials for assisted-living places on TV. In those fantastical sixty-second segments, a daughter sits with her aged father who's happy to look at old photos together all day, or she gently holds her mom's hand, walking slowly to somewhere lovely, her mom happily and peacefully going along. It's all serenity and special moments. What a bunch of baloney. Picture-perfect fakery eats families alive from the inside. It keeps us isolated and prepares us for nothing—as with addiction, and pretty much everything else in life, too. We need to hear and see honest stories.

*There's a long line of worn and ragged people trudging
down the road, slowly weaving their way in my direction,
returning from the front lines. Stooped and weary, aged
by the experience of years. They've been there. They've seen
things. Shell-shocked and battle-fatigued. I can see it in
their eyes.*

*I stand in silent honor, not wanting to intrude on their
thoughts, on their efforts to make it back home where
it's safe. I'm hungry for their knowledge about ~~addiction~~*
Alzheimer disease and aging, *to learn what they've learned
about how to help, not hurt, my ~~child~~* **parents.** *I'm hungry
to know how to survive. Things I've not yet learned.*

*When the time is right, they will tell their tale—in little
trickles or with floodgates open wide. They will share their
war stories, their lessons, so that my own time in hell will
be a little less prolonged. A little less harrowing. A little less
hard. Their stories might shake my world, but they will also
give me realistic expectations and fill me with hope. To those
people who've walked this road before me, I give my respect
and thanks. To them, I tip my hat.*

—*Tending Dandelions,* 195

•

*Mom, I love you, have always loved you, and have always
known how much you love me. And even though I've been
so mad at you sometimes, I now understand that everything
you've been doing, you've been doing for me.*

My heart swoons. Joey has put into words what I've always
known (even when I sometimes didn't). My son loves me and sees
my love for him in action, even when The Addict—who some-

times runs the show—doesn't. These are the words I have ached to hear for the past ten years, and they are words I will hold tight to forever.

Joey and I continue to replenish the stuff of our bond, dusting off the cobwebs with frequent texts and periodic phone calls. A connection of love, both fragile and strong at the same time. A mother-son connection we both need. With a forged history behind us, we rarely talk about anything having to do with addiction; by unspoken agreement, we use our time to make pleasant new memories to hold on to. It's our connection of love that matters.

My book *Tending Dandelions* was just recently released. When we were in Minnesota a few months ago, I mentioned my soon-to-be-published new book to Joey, along with a brief description. But I won't mention it again. He didn't have anything to say about it then, and if he wants to know more about it or my mission, he will ask. And, truly, whether he knows or asks or not, changes are happening.

I will be open about what addiction has done to my child and family. I will speak the truth with my head held high. Even among—especially among—people who look at me with disdain and discomfort. There's nothing shameful about addiction—the only shame is in allowing the disease to grow by hiding the truth in the darkness. Ignorance, ugly words, and harsh judgment end where education begins. So, as the mom of an addict, I must do my part in planting the seeds of truth and understanding.

I am not a bad mom; my son is not a bad person. Addiction is a disease that can happen to anyone who opens Pandora's box. I will honor my son by changing the way addiction is perceived.

Seeds are being planted. In some of the places those seeds land, they will actually grow. And, in time, they will spread more seeds. Truth. And enlightenment. Like fluffy tufts of dandelion caught on the wind.

—*Tending Dandelions,* 169

I have found my calling, my purpose, as a voice for mothers with addicted children, helping to put an end to the shame and silence, and helping my son in the only way I can. With my writing and public speaking, I have found a career—and healing.

I'm getting ready for a presentation to a parents' group in Maryland in a few days—followed by a few days in court where I will come face-to-face with Josh and his latest whim. Back to the state where our divorce was filed. I'm trying to tamp down my worry that the judge will decide in favor of Josh's career change (hence the need to reduce alimony) and shove my budding career off its track. I'm trying to be hopeful that *right* will win. While printing piles of papers to tuck in my suitcase along with way too many outfits, in pops a text from a friend, the latest one in a string of texts we've been exchanging: *Have you thought about getting a real job? I'm not saying what you do doesn't have value. But you could do something you're passionate about and earn an income at the same time.*

Me: *I work really hard, every day, helping people who love someone suffering with the disease of addiction. I do what I do for them, for Joey, and for me. I feel it's a huge accomplishment to have been published three times; it's too bad being an author doesn't pay well, but that wasn't the point back when I got started. I can't even imagine being forced into doing something random and meaning-less instead of continuing with this thing I've built out of nothing but life experience and passion, on my own, step by step, over* the past decade. I can't imagine cutting off the bud before it has a chance to bloom.

Friend: *Keep the faith. When one door closes another one opens.*

Me: *It's sad that the person who keeps closing my doors is the one who once supposedly loved me.*

I understand that to Josh, I've become *someone that he used to know.* A ball and chain in his rearview mirror. And to me, *he's* become a cliché of the male divorcé. Hoping to touch some bit of the man I used to know, I've written Josh a letter (which turns out to be more of a kick in the pants). He'll probably never read it, but I needed to try one last time to make him see the ramifications of what he's doing for *himself* on *me.*

> *Josh,*
>
> *You built our relationship on a big lie—on a secret only you knew—treating me as a stepping stone and taking away my chance at giving my love to someone who would love me back, forever.*
>
> *You built your life on my future.*
>
> *Until you were done—leaving me to figure out the rest of my life, all alone.*
>
> *You didn't unveil your secret with integrity—a secret you could've, should've shared long before you were finally forced to be honest. Instead, you left me to wait, wonder, hope, and smother for years. You had a smooth uncorking, at least within our family; you had nothing but love and support from me because I cared about you. It turns out that all you've cared about is you, too.*
>
> *For so long, I was flailing around trying to figure out what was happening, and then, once I knew, I started trying to figure out how to stand—but you've kept pulling my rug out*

from under me. Again and again and again. Now, this time, by removing my financial security, taking away the life I've built (both comfortable and conservative), on the promise you made, five years ago.

Somehow, you've been able to disregard the fact that I haven't worked for thirty years, other than raising our family and supporting your career from its first lowly rung. But I'm now facing the very scary prospect of trying to earn a livable wage at age fifty-eight (without any of that nice spousal support). In order to pay my bills and keep my house, I will need to abandon the career I've been working on—helping other parents on the path we've been on for so long—and figure something else out. So, while you enjoy the job security and benefits of working for companies owned by your husband (and having a well-employed husband), my life will be re-duced to merely working to live.

I'm not stupid. I know you wouldn't continue pursuing a career in which you have no hope of being successful. I know we are where we are because you're choosing to sacrifice me in order to maintain a certain level of extravagance for you. I'm just hoping you'll be moved to do what's right.

Your legacy continues—your boys continue to watch and learn. I'm sad for them, I'm sad for me, and I'm even a little sad for you.

On the day our alimony modification trial begins, a full year after Josh preemptively modified it, I wake up way too early, roused by a sense of doom. Nothing I packed in my suitcase a few days ago seems right for the occasion now that it's here, and my knees are quaking. Bonnie, the friend I'm staying with, drives me to the courthouse and will stay with me for moral support through the days ahead. After parking the car and figuring out where we're supposed to go, we step into the opening doors of an elevator, and there is Josh, wrapping up a business call. He then aims his jovial warmth toward us. My face, my mouth, my neck, my brain, my heart—they're all working at the same time to do the best they can in a split-second battle between politeness and a slew of conflicting emotions. I can see in the reflection of the shiny elevator walls that I look like a caricature of something human. Bonnie, I can tell, doesn't feel the same need to be polite.

When Josh and I were divorced, it was through a process of mediation, so the only times I've been in a courtroom before were when Joey was in some sort of trouble—and then, Josh was sitting with me on the same side. Shoulder to shoulder, hand in hand. Today, we are on opposite sides of the rows of wooden benches, seated in swivel chairs at long tables up front, our lawyers positioned between us—not that Josh and I need such safeguarding, but clearly something happened to someone at some time in the past that cemented this as standard operating procedure. The judge sits up front in her black robe, elevated, like the witness stand, where each of us will recite the oath of truth.

Behind us, other than Bonnie, the courtroom is empty besides a few paralegals and the woman who performed a vocational assessment on me back in Texas a few months ago. She's here to testify that, at my age and with my lack of work experience, I can basically expect to earn minimum wage—similar to the other assessment Josh's team had done, before the divorce, too. A discussion ensues on jobs that might be suitable for me—to which I can only listen: *She could go back to school and get recertified as an elementary school teacher, but would anyone want to hire a rusty old relic when there are fresh young teachers churning out of colleges every year?* (If anyone cares, I don't want to go back to teaching after thirty years out of the classroom, even *if* schools wanted me.) *She could take classes to become a computer programmer.* (Something I know nothing about and so care nothing about embracing as my twilight career.) *Why couldn't she be a hostess at a restaurant?* asks the judge, to which the vocational assessment lady replies, *Well, then she'd be earning even less.*

My value, my future, are reduced to a few minutes of negotiation by strangers. Josh's future, too, but it's quite apparent the judge thinks he needs to maintain a certain level of panache to project *success* to his clients. Panache, for me, isn't even on the table. The opinion and order of the court will be revealed within a few months. I return to Texas feeling squashed. Worthless and hopeless. Tired of pulling myself up by my bootstraps with nothing more than sheer willpower over and over again.

> *"Get it together," they say. "Pull yourself up by the bootstraps and start moving again." Or "Turn your frown upside down." Some version or another of "Stop moping around."*
>
> *They say this as though I'm not working on this very thing all day, every day. As though I'm a weakling just sitting around munching on misery bonbons instead. They have no idea how many times I've stooped over, grabbed those very heavy bootstraps they're talking about, and wearily hoisted myself back up—if they* did, *they'd know I'm actually pretty strong. I've had to dig really deep, over and over and over again, to pull myself out of each crisis-induced slump. That's what a mom does when her child is slowly dying from addiction.*
>
> *They say I look tired. But it's not because I've given up. It's because I've been doing heavy lifting, daily, for years.*
>
> —*"Bootstraps," Readings for Moms of Addicts*

I feel bad my friends are stuck with me as a friend—the friend with the never-ending messes clinging like some icky toxic waste. Sometimes I feel like how Pigpen must feel, Charlie Brown's dusty little friend, if he weren't just a cartoon. He's not a gloomy guy, but the traveling dust storm he generates is enough to keep people away; no one wants the dirt to rub off. I don't want to *be* that friend. But I *am* that friend. So I go into hiding till I'm able to slap on a happy face. I mow and mulch and mull things over till I've got my feelings and thoughts mostly worked out and/or contained.

And then I dive into the things where healing really happens—the things that involve helping someone else who's hurting in one way or another. This is how I survive. I find healing in writing my books and speaking with other moms with addicted children and in cooking with the girls at the maternity home. This week we're making breakfast for dinner, stretching the girls' skills and food exploration, as always: blueberry French toast roll-ups, scrambled egg hash brown cups, spiced maple sausage patties, and sweet potato and kale veggie cakes. I know these weekly cooking adventures aren't going to change the world, but I also know that little things can also be big. The time the girls and I spend together is relaxed and fun, and it is *this* that might be even more valuable than any cooking skills they might learn. *"When I do good I feel good."* I don't know who said this, but for me it's very true.

> *I'm learning to live without my child, but, like someone whose leg has been amputated, through force of habit I often reach for the place he once was. The pain I feel is not phantom. If I'm to survive, the void left behind must be filled with some goodness.*

> *There's so much hurt in the world—hurt is happening all around me, not only within me. There are other lost parents*

who are missing a lost child. And the children who are lost.
There are lost souls who are hungry, lonely, or running on
empty. I don't need to look very far to find ways to turn my
pain into purpose. Ways to be constructive. Productive.
Ways to help keep others from breaking, even as I mend
my own self.

I can hold a hand, lend an ear, and watch over with care.
For them. For me. But also, in honor of my child. Addiction
has hacked my child from my life, but he will be with me
every step of the way as I move forward.

—*Tending Dandelions,* 189

In preparation for my long-planned *Where Love and Addiction Meet* speaking tour, I'm packing my suitcase full of sweaters and cute autumn boots. Starting tomorrow, I'll spend the next two weeks talking with a dozen different groups from New York to Virginia . . . because, well, *together we are stronger.* Then, since I'll already be in Rick's neck of the woods, he and I are going to spend Thanksgiving together in New York City.

Rick's NYC apartment is tiny (tiny tiny tiny), so I stay in a nearby hotel—a costly drawback to visiting my son here. But there's also so much to see and do, and Rick indulges his tourist mom. On Thanksgiving Eve, we walk among the giant balloons being inflated in the streets of Manhattan for tomorrow's parade—Charlie Brown, Olaf from *Frozen*, Tom Turkey—all coming to life, bobbing around under nets weighted with sandbags to keep them from blowing away before morning. We go to look at the enchanting department store holiday window displays, and then, once I realize where we are, I take a photo of Rick standing under the street sign on the corner—*my miracle on 34th Street.* I'm so thankful for him. We meet friends of mine in a restaurant for Thanksgiving dinner—the first time we've not had Thanksgiving dinner in a home. It's different, nontraditional, but it's nice. We're getting adept at adapting.

Rick will be with his dad for Christmas this year, so I'll go to Golden Valley to see my parents. Mom has rallied, is no longer receiving hospice care, and she and Dad are happy and doing really well, all things considered. (Whew.) Last year, I thought I was being so clever, getting Rick to help me wrap my decorated tree with Saran Wrap after the holiday was over—round and round and round we went, poking in the renegade ornaments trying to escape. I figured that since decorating and undecorating a Christmas tree isn't much fun alone, and since I live in a one-story house where it would be easy to push a Christmas tree on wheels from a closet to the living room and vice versa, this genius idea I read about seemed worth a try. But I won't be rolling the tree out or putting up any other decorations this year. It's not worth the bother.

It has taken a few months, but the judge has finally, officially made her decision on my alimony, but I knew in the courtroom how this was going to shake out. *I've lost.* Nobody cared what I've been up to all these years, helping others who love a child suffering with addiction while honoring my son at the same time; nobody cared about the work or the time I've put in, or the connections and accomplishments I've made. Nobody cared about my purpose, my reason to live, my need to move beyond that pain and turn it into something positive. Nobody *cared.* And nobody *cares.* It matters to nobody involved what comes next for me—what this decision means for how I will spend my days or afford the rest of my life. Nobody will ever give it a second thought.

I've lost yet another thing to which I've given everything: my career. I will need to find a *real* job.

●

Christmas in Minnesota is *co-o-o-ld*. I can't imagine how anyone lives in this state. With windchill, every day is some crazy below-zero number. The car I've rented has heated seats—a feature I have in my own car in Texas but never need to use—and it also has a heated steering wheel(!). A newfangled invention (to me). These northerners know how to do *cold* right. Me, not so much. I left a bottle of red wine in the car overnight, something to take to the friends having my dad and me for Christmas dinner, but there was a long wine popsicle on the back-seat floor when I went to slip it into a gift bag. Oops.

Mom is back to her old after-dementia-before-hospice-care self, zipping around her one-room domain and happily giving orders, and Dad is cheerfully comfortable in his daily routine (which sometimes still requires us kids to intervene). Their old home and life are just fuzzy memories now. I guess they've settled in rather quickly—even though it seemed like they never would—after having lived together in one place for nearly forever. So adaptable. And full of positivity. Dad says, "You know, I'd rather be home, but this place is really nice. I don't think anyone *couldn't* be happy here." Well, I think plenty of people could find reasons to be miserable about where they are, what they've lost, and what could've, should've been, but Mom and Dad are happy.

I'm the one who's not.

Instead of staying with my brother or friends, as I've been doing since Mom and Dad moved out of their house, I'm staying in a hotel. I don't want to impose on anyone's special family time for a whole week at the holidays. And I need space to cry.

Soft carols float through the hotel lobby, following the families laden with gifts and good cheer in and out the revolving door. I pretend to be *one of them*, hanging a smile on my face like a crooked decoration as we all come and go. I pretend all is Christmas-letter perfect for my parents, too. But in my heart, I'm a Scrooge. I don't know when I will be able to see my parents again. Or Rick in New York. Or Joey in Florida, now that we've reconnected. Flying is no longer in my budget, and none of my most special people live close enough to Texas for me to drive. The *people who do not care* have made it really difficult for me to see the *people who do* going forward. Making me even more alone than I was.

Nothing is as it should be. And for so many years—all at once, one by one, and overlapping—nothing was as it appeared. Truth and illusions, illness and meanness. What and who was real. I don't know what lies ahead—I don't even really know what happened behind me.

·

If I were to fill my watering can and pour it over a prized flower in my garden, the water would not only feed that one thirsty flower—the water would overflow into the surrounding spaces, seeping into the soil and roots, feeding the flowers nearby. That's how self-care works, too. Just as with a prized flower in my garden, a bit of watering can (and will) make my soul grow and bloom—benefiting not only myself, but everyone around me.

If I were to fill my watering can and pour it over me, filling myself to the brim with kindness—with patience and acceptance, permission and opportunity—I would be treating myself the way I deserve to be treated by everyone else. If I were to drench my mind and heart with hope, peace, and joy, I would feel fulfilled, not drained. That's how self-care works: just as with a prized flower in my garden, a bit of watering can (and will) make my soul grow and bloom—everything good that is possible begins, and flows, from within me.

—"Watering Can (and Will)"
Readings for Moms of Addicts

I've been thinking.

And feeling.

A lot.

For the past several months, before heading out to find a bearable new job and life—a *real* job with value—I've been wrapping up some commitments, things I'd been working on long before the alimony decision was made—a "Mom to Mom" retreat at Hazelden (their first retreat for moms with addicted children, ever) and a few other speaking events up in Minnesota (so I was able to see my folks, too).

I've been slowly letting go of one thread so I can pick up the next.

In the midst of this process—the thinking, the feeling, the wrapping up—I've discovered that I can't abandon my life's purpose, with both my career and my family. Like Dad, whose purpose continues in heart-muscle memory, I might wither and die if I had to give it all up. My purpose is *who I am,* hatched from the life I've lived and the choices I've made, and I can't allow my purpose to be controlled by the bombshells and roadblocks and pigeonholes of uncaring others.

I want to be *better* not *bitter.* I want to be more happy than sad. So I'm going to believe in myself and take control of my destiny. I'm going to try spinning a pile of straw into something golden. (Fingers crossed that it works.)

I've decided to move back to Minnesota, the place where I have the most addiction-related connections, the most family, and the most old, old friends. The place where I have the most options, relationships, and likelihood of all-around success. The threads of Golden Valley, all the years wrapped like roots around my heart and soul, are pulling me back.

I choose to be happy.

When you choose joy, you feel good. When you feel good, you do good. And when you do good, it reminds others of what joy feels like and it might inspire them to do the same.

—UNKNOWN

Part Three

Better, Not Worse

It is what it is.
But it will become
what you make it.

—UNKNOWN

Of Roots and Wings

"What good are wings without the courage to fly?"

—ATTICUS FINCH IN *TO KILL A MOCKINGBIRD* BY HARPER LEE

"MINNESOTA WELCOMES YOU!"

I smile to myself as the huge state-shaped sign at the side of the freeway comes into view, welcoming me home. *Home.* It has taken forty long years—topped off by a long drive from Austin, Texas—to get here. But with this move, I'm uprooting the roots I keep replanting for the very last time.

Just two months ago, at the end of August, I put my most recent *forever home* (of four years) up for sale. Within a few days it was under contract, so everything that has happened since has happened really fast. In a hastily organized house-hunting trip, I found my new home-to-be about thirty minutes out from the suburb where I grew up. An area of wetlands and rolling hills, dotted with small lakes, silos, and old barns with big, square, hand-painted heirloom-quilt patterns on one side, it is quaint, quiet, and beautiful. When I discovered this place, I felt a sense of serenity, of healing, and I decided to plant myself there. I found a house that is now under construction—the builders have just broken ground—which means I won't have to worry about unexpected expenses like a new roof or old plumbing for the rest of my days, but it will be several months until I can move in, so I'll be staying in an extended-stay hotel until February.

I've moved so many times—dozens—but never under such a tight deadline. So, after finding somewhere for me to move in, I spent my remaining weeks in Texas getting ready for the movers to move me out. While building ever-growing piles of empty tape rolls and stacks of heavy boxes, there was little time for anything else. When Dad had a stroke, I had to keep on packing, knowing that Thomas was with him and I would be there soon. When cooking with the girls at the maternity home for the last time, much sooner than expected, I said my goodbyes believing that the years we had together mattered, even if they weren't nearly enough. And when saying goodbye to my friends, precious moments squeezed in like another carefully wrapped dish into a box, I comforted myself with the knowledge that true friendships endure no matter the distance.

And then, three days ago, after the movers loaded all of my things onto their truck and hauled them off to storage—after mopping my way out my front door and signing the papers to close on the sale of my house—I climbed into my car parked in front of the strip mall closing office, packed to the roof with things I might need over the next months, and started driving north. From Texas to Oklahoma, Kansas to Missouri, and now, finally, from Iowa to Minnesota, I've been putting on warmer clothes in each state. In Texas, the days before Halloween may still feel like summer, but up here there's a chill in the October air that feels more like winter to me.

I was nervous about making this drive all alone; up till now, on long trips I've always had a copilot. I'm still haunted sometimes by a car accident I had years ago. The accident was all my fault—

I was speeding because I was running late to pick someone up from the airport because our dog was more focused on sniffing than doing his business. (You can take a dog to every tree in the neighborhood, but you can't make him pee.) I was driving much faster than the 120 km/h (75 mph) speed limit on the *autovía* in Spain, but the roadway was empty except for one small speck far ahead in the distance. I felt comfortable glancing away for a second to rummage through my purse on the seat next to me in an immediate need to refresh my lipstick. Glancing back up, the speck in the distance was suddenly a slow-moving car *right* in front of me. I swerved into the left lane, then back to the right, avoiding hitting the other car but overcorrecting, veering wildly back and forth, back and forth. In high-speed slow motion. I remember being aware that I wasn't going to get my car under control; I remember being grateful my boys were safe at school and not with me; and I remember knowing I was going to die.

Then, sometime later, I was hanging upside down, held in place by my seatbelt, my head partially scalped by the broken metal frame of the convertible top—which, because I'd wanted my hair to look cute when I arrived at the airport, had not been down. Somehow, I arrived at the hospital and was stitched up like a baseball, eventually returning home half-bald, with a fractured neck, broken wrist, and minor lacerations on my face. My car had slammed into a cement wall, flipped, and rolled, but my injuries finally healed, and I was left with no residual effects other than gratefulness for the way things turned out—things could have been so much worse in *so* many ways. And, of course, gratefulness for a second chance—*the meaning of life* was forever changed.

Sometimes though, even after all these years, I still have to dig deep and make a determined decision not to allow myself to be paralyzed by the fear of driving on highways alone—especially now that I *am* alone. I can't allow fear to sabotage my life. So now, driving over the state line from Iowa to Minnesota, the last leg of the longest solo expedition of my life, I'm not only excited about being here—I also feel like I've just conquered something *big.*

Stopping at the first gas station I come to, I fill up my tank, feeling a little giddy about my new life ahead in the state where my feet have finally touched ground as a new resident. Grabbing a cup of coffee for the road, I smile and say *you betcha!* to the cashier when she sends me on my way with a friendly *have a good day!* Just one hundred miles to go.

When my boys were little, we lived in a town not too far from here—the last time we ever lived anywhere near family, and for only a year. Rick was still a baby and Joey had just turned three when a Halloween blizzard blew in, an early start to a winter that seemingly lasted forever. At the time, we had only one car, so early every morning, I would stuff the boys into their snowsuits and mittens before carrying them to the car and stuffing them into car seats so we could take Josh to work. A pair of little puffballs, Rick could barely wiggle his arms that stuck out sort of sideways, and Joey would tip over after a few teetering steps and just lie there, too hot and tuckered out to get back up. After a certain number of tears (not only mine), I decided the three of us would be happier just staying in the house for the next half a year; winter from the Mom perspective was not the same fun I remembered having as a kid. So, when Josh's next promotion took us to Houston, I meant it when I said I would never, ever, live in Minnesota again.

But, now, all these years later, here I am. And winter is just around the corner. It seems that the warmth of deep roots can thaw out even the most icy of declarations.

There's comfort in knowing I will be near family and old

friends—near people I've known forever, with whom I have a shared history. Once Josh and the boys moved on, I no longer had that, and the *alone* I've been doing has been *too alone;* I want to feel the vibes of enduring connection floating around in my airspace. I need something solid behind me, something I will probably never need to lean on, but the presence of which practically guarantees that I won't—sort of like the three Xanax tablets I've had tucked away in my purse for the past ten years, ever since my anxiety attack while on the hunt for a new home and life in Asheville, North Carolina. Untouched and long expired, they're there if I need them, but because I know they're there, I don't. It is the knowing that is enough.

My roots—the early years of figuring out the world and the people I was figuring out the world with—are wrapped like so many threads around the person I've become.

When my parents allowed me to work out my spats with friends or my mess-ups at school, I was learning diplomacy and problem-solving and personal responsibility—and the power of believing in my own ability to get things done. When my brothers did things like hide under the bed to grab my ankles just as I was climbing in for a peaceful night's sleep, I learned (eventually) that it's possible to love people even when you don't like them very much, and (eventually) the art of forgiveness. And when I pushed a friend off the edge of a playground structure for no reason at all, I learned the art of being forgiven (also eventually).

On Christmas Eve, when my cousins, brothers, and I would press our noses to the front window at Grandma's house, watching for Santa to walk up her sidewalk with his big bag full of gifts, I was learning about magical moments, and then keeping good secrets, and then how to deal with it when someone blabbed. And, when we would huddle together at the bottom of the creaky wooden stairs to Grandma's attic looking up at the rattly skeleton from Dad's medical school days dangling from a pole on the landing—a skeleton we'd have to squeeze by in order to play with the world's most beautiful dollhouse—I was learning about courage, giving comfort, sharing, and the pros and cons of taking scary chances.

On winter evenings, when skating with cousins as graceful as gazelles (while my own movements were more like Fred Flintstone starting his car), I was learning the difference between wishes and goals, and that betterment doesn't happen by magic—but I was also learning that magic *does* happen when sharing hot chocolate with warm company. When digging igloos in the mounds of snow at the end of the driveway—wearing Wonder Bread bags under my boots (to keep my feet dry) and eating the teeny snowball-ettes attached to my red wool mittens (to keep my hands dry)—I was learning about teamwork, hard work, and that motivation can keep even a fake-fur-trimmed Popsicle moving.

When skipping down the street to the school bus with friends, or saving a seat at the lunch table, or trying out a new fashion trend, I was learning about loyalty, honesty, diplomacy, and the power of friendship's comforting shield. When playing Capture the Flag or Monopoly, I was learning about fair play, conflict resolution, and the art of graceful winning and losing. And when sharing all the *firsts* (and *nexts*) as they unrolled over the years—periods, crushes, broken hearts, and dreams—I was learning trust and empathy, new ways to do stuff (and how not to do stuff), and the importance of being true to myself.

Now, at the end of my long drive, pulling my car into the hotel parking lot, my home-before-home for the next several months, I feel the energy—both quiet and strong—of my roots. I know there's risk in this move (since I've been trying to find my place in the world for the past ten years and haven't gotten it right yet), but now I'm back at the nourishing source. The place where my roots sprouted wings.

The hotel isn't fancy, but it's cheap and not too far from my folks—and I'll only be here for a few months (but too long to impose on family or friends). The lobby is small, with only two chairs, so there's no place for me to *be* except my room, so I plan to be anywhere else as much as possible. I've hauled my boxes and suitcases from the car, unpacking only the essentials and stacking everything else in the corner. There's a queen bed, a comfy chair, and a small kitchenette where I can cook simple meals, but I'm storing my food and dishes on the counter and hanging my garbage on the doorknob, because the insides of the cupboards are too cruddy to ever open again. There's a door right across the hall from my door, a small trash room with three garbage cans that becomes one big oozing dumpster on weekends, so I only open that door between Tuesday and Friday. But the person at the front desk is always nice, and I have a housekeeper that comes once a week to change the sheets and clean the bathroom, so I'm enjoying that, and the free internet, while it lasts.

Mom and Dad are happy I'm here, although I'm not sure they grasp that I'm here to stay. If my spirits ever need a boost, I just need to show up at Mom's door (even when I'm already visiting her and had only stepped out into the hall for a minute). Every. Single. Time. She greets me with *such joy* that the moment is a gift to both of us. Dad's stroke last month didn't affect his mobility, but it did affect part of his brain and left him unable to read—he can still write, *but can't read what he wrote;* the human brain is a weird place. He's getting some sort of therapy, and hopefully it will help, because Dad loves to read; he *needs* to read. And he is very proud. For now, when we're at a restaurant and the waiter hands us some menus, I read out loud the things I know Dad might like, saying, "I think I might order the tuna sandwich on toasted wheat bread. Or maybe I'll have the Reuben. Also, the homemade chicken noodle soup sounds good to me," so he can choose what to eat without having to ask.

Since I'm a *local* now, my visits with Mom and Dad are much different than they've ever been; they're regular and spontaneous pop-ins instead of well-planned weeklong or monthlong visits that were the norm for all the decades since I left. I'm so grateful for this time—this different sort of time—but I wish it had happened sooner, back when we could have real conversations and meetings of the mind. I miss that part of our connection, even though we still always have meetings of the heart.

Meetings of the heart. Often, that's the only connection I have with Joey and Rick, too. They're both far away—but their love stays with me, and I draw strength from that. And the belief that it works *the other way around* keeps me going. I feel and know Joey's and Rick's love, and I know that Joey and Rick feel and know mine, no matter what. The same applies to Mom and Dad.

Love is the connection, even when connection on another level isn't possible, for whatever reason.

Dementia. Miles. Or addiction.

Pablo Picasso once said, "Only put off until tomorrow what you are willing to die having left undone." I could put a lot of things in the pile of nonessentials: cleaning my garage, washing my car, stepping on the bathroom scale, trying exotic foods like alligator-tail tacos or turtle soup. But there's a big ol' pile of things that I would regret—very much—if I left them undone. And letting my loved ones know that I love them is on the top of the heap.

I know they already know it. I know they all know they're loved beyond reason. I know that. I do. But, what if today is such a rough day that they don't? So, I will say I love you *every chance I get. If I can't say* I love you *with words, I will say it with actions. And if I can't do that, I'll find a way to fling an* I love you *over the miles in some unorthodox manner; it doesn't matter how the message gets there . . . it just has to get there.*

There's always tomorrow. *Except when there isn't.*

I love you, I love you, I love you.

—*Tending Dandelions,* 219

·

Thanksgiving. I miss the way it used to be, back when my kids and anyone else we could cram around the table would join together for the big feast. I miss the planning and decorating and cooking—I miss pulling together a menu with everyone's favorites and creating a centerpiece with hand-gilded gourds, and making a gravy that is mostly lump-less and seasoned just right. I love filling my house with family and friends, pulling everyone together for feast and fun—and I miss the weeks of heightened anticipation and excitement leading up to that. I miss what used to be my whole *Thanksgiving package* and probably always will. But I'm grateful to have been included in the long-established traditions of family and friends over the past years—and again this year, too.

Since Mom is most comfortable within the four walls of her studio apartment, Dad, Thomas, his kids, and I join her while she eats her Thanksgiving meal, and then I take Dad to have Thanksgiving dinner with longtime friends. Friends as comfortable as old slippers. Friends who were his neighbors for fifty years, from the time their daughter and I were in kindergarten up until the time Mom and Dad needed to move. Sitting around the table now, surrounded by this gaggle of his generation and mine, I'm grateful for the long-lasting connection—for all of us. A connection that *connects* even with the ongoing evolution of aging.

Friends like family and family like friends. Today, on Thanksgiving, I'm giving thanks for the bottomless gift of that.

I have so much to be thankful for, really. Dad and I have been taking weekly field trips to see the progress on my new house, sharing our amazement at how quickly a hole in the ground has taken wood-framed shape. I've been earning a little extra income as a substitute lunch lady at my old elementary school (a leap back in time, where everything is much tinier than remembered). I've been working on another "Mom to Mom" retreat to be held in the spring. And I've signed a contract for my next book, *Just Dandy*—my journey of stumbling through so much, all at once. A journey so many women share. I'm starting to outline the chapters now, and I will start the real writing once I'm moved into my new house.

In the days before Christmas, I take Dad to the mall so he can get Mom a box of her favorite chocolates (her favorite food) and out for a drive to view some of the most spectacular holiday light displays in the area. I map out a half-dozen homes with animated snowmen, reindeer, and Santas arranged across snowy yards and snowy roofs, all brightly lit and choreographed to music we tune in to on the car radio as we slowly drive by. Also, I'm getting a hotel room ready for Rick's weeklong visit, just down the hall from mine. It's a corner room and quite a bit bigger, with a bigger bed and windows on two sides instead of just one, so I greedily contemplate taking it for myself, but the thought of moving all my stuff again quickly snuffs out that idea. I'm happy enough and settled in where I am. I don't put up a Christmas tree, not even a tabletop version like Mom and Dad each have—it seems silly to pretend there's anything traditional about Christmas this year—so I decorate Rick's room with big red ribbons, hang his stocking (that I packed and brought along), and fill his kitchenette countertop with snacks. This seems just right.

Rick likes my new house-to-be, such as it is, which currently has plywood floors and walls and windows. Jonathan and his California crew are here for the holiday, too, and join us for my *and the sofa will go here* tour. It's easier now for everyone to be in one place, with one fewer of us siblings needing to travel. I drop unsubtle hints to Rick, as usual, about him moving closer (to my *state* not my *house*). I don't see that happening anytime soon, if ever, but he likes *cold and snowy* better than *hot and more hot,* so the chance of him moving to Minnesota is probably better than the chance of him moving to Texas was. But no matter where Rick lives for the rest of his years, I want him to feel rooted to something beyond just the place he plants himself. I'm not at all sure that roots, even happy roots, can survive the ripping apart of a family, so I want Rick—and hopefully, someday, Joey, too—to feel a sense of grounding here.

On Christmas morning, Rick and I visit Mom and Dad, carrying in some gifts and goodies and good cheer. I put a holiday headband on Mom's head, adorned with two bobbling snowmen and a flourish of tinsel. Thomas has already been here, leaving a gift of neon pink eyeglasses trimmed with long, dark eyelashes on the upper rim, and Mom can't pull together this new ensemble fast enough. Slipping on her robe, the one with lamb ears on the hood, she hurries out of her room, saying the other gifts can wait. *C'mon!* The rest of us follow along as she marches up and down the hallway, walking up to everyone she sees, waiting for comments—thoroughly, but oh so joyously, out of her previously reserved character. She stops in front of two ladies perched on a cushioned bench. Beaming. Posing. "So what do you think?" she asks. Holding her four-foot-nine self tall, sparkling from inside and out. They both stare at Mom for a few moments before one leans toward the other and says, "What's different? Her shoes?" I see more holiday headbands in Mom's future.

Rick says he thinks this version of his grandma is cute, although he's probably also thinking (with dread) about what changes lie ahead for me—what unpredictable directions my personality might take—down the road. I'm thinking about what he's thinking because I'm thinking about all of this, too.

On New Year's Day, after dropping Rick off at the airport to catch his flight back to New York, I pick up Dad and we go out for lunch to kick off the new year. Over turkey sandwiches and chips, he talks about old times and the old house, so after we're finished eating, we go for a drive through the old neighborhood. Tires crunching on the snow, I pull over to the deeply buried curb and put the car into park so we can gaze at what used to be *home* for a few minutes. Still painted yellow with black shutters, the house looks pretty much the same, but *less vital* somehow now that Mom and Dad are no longer in it. A squirrel hops through the fluffy snow and then up the trunk and into the bare branches of the towering maple tree in the middle of the front yard. I ask Dad if remembers whose tree that is—one of three trees he planted as a living ode to each of us kids when we were little. He doesn't remember, and neither do I. But it doesn't matter.

Each of those trees grew strong and tall on the same patch of ground as Thomas, Jonathan, and I grew up on, too—withstanding storms, providing shade, and putting on quite a show with the change of each season—and they might even outlive us all. But no matter what, the roots will remain, because the roots planted here live within each of us kids, threads of a lifetime, tying us together. Mom and Dad's roots are my roots. I'm so lucky. (I wish I could believe that Rick and Joey feel the same way about their roots, too.)

> *My family and friends have helped so much in getting me through tough times. I couldn't have made it to today without them. But I've learned that there isn't always going to be somebody around when I need support; my main support network needs to be what goes on inside my own head. I need to be my own first line of defense. I need to rely on myself, not someone else, to hold myself up.*
>
> *I need to trust in myself. I can trust in myself. I have shown myself over and over again that I can rise up to the lowest occasion. I can count on myself to do the right thing when the wrong thing hits the fan. I can emerge from the darkest of places—still somewhat put together—all in one piece.*
>
> *When and if the world is pulled out from under me again, I won't fall flat on my face. My family and friends have helped me so much to find strength. I now have the belief in myself—the wind beneath my own wings—I need to soar.*
>
> —Tending Dandelions, 149

Minnesotans know how to do winter right. They embrace it. They *own* it. They make it fun. I'm sure I'll get there eventually—all gung-ho and making cold things happen—but at this point I'm just happy to tag along. I've bundled up and joined my cousins for an evening stroll across the meandering frozen lakes in Minneapolis, oohing and aahing over the spectacular ice sculptures glittering with lights, the fire and ice dancers, and the musical performance played on instruments created from ice. I've bundled up and joined friends for an evening stroll through the arboretum, stopping to make s'mores around a bonfire before continuing the tour of enchanting light displays throughout the winter gardens. I've bundled up both me and my dad and joined friends on an evening stroll through an ice castle built from thousands of icicles, with frozen thrones, tunnels, and fountains. The winter is cold, but it can be a wonderland, and the people here keep it warmed up.

Unsurprisingly (but still shockingly), the official move into my new house was delayed a few days because the February windchill of *fifty degrees below zero* was too cold for the movers to move my stuff in. But I moved myself and my boxes anyway, right after the closing, not at all sad to scrape the snow and ice off the windshield of my car in the hotel parking lot for the last time. Having bought an air mattress and borrowed linens from friends, I used a cardboard box as a table, turned on the gas fireplace, and ordered a pizza, happy to be basking in the warmth of my new home that first night. It looked pretty darn good, considering I had selected all the finishes—the floors, paint colors, cabinetry, exterior siding, etc.—within a three-hour window back in August, after which there was no turning back. Pretty. Darn. Good.

Now, one month after moving in, just as I'm unpacking the last box and arranging the spice drawer, opportunity knocks in the most wonderful way. Many months ago, I proposed an idea to my editor at Hazelden about creating a website—a dynamic, vital, and easy-to-navigate online hub for moms with addicted children. Today that idea—MomPower.org—is given wings:

> *By moms and for moms, MomPower.org is dedicated to educating and empowering moms with addicted children. We're here to connect you with everything you might need to find strength, wisdom, perspective, sanity, and hope during a*

*most confusing and scary time. We're here to help you come
to understand addiction as a disease, not a moral or parental failure. Not a disgrace. Helping you to put the stigma,
shame, blame, guilt and silence behind you so that healing
may begin.*

*One by one and one after another, we're helping moms with
addicted children to change the way addiction is perceived—
in our homes, in our communities, and in the reflection our
beloved children see in our eyes. Together we are changing the
dynamic of the place where love and addiction meet. And
together we are stronger.*

Just a small team of three, a web person, a marketing person, and
myself, we have two months to get the website ready for a Mother's
Day launch. My job is to know what needs to be included and
to gather it up—articles to be written by other moms, support
groups and parent coaching, ways to take action, books and pod-
casts, a national calendar of events, and much more. I can picture
the whole website in my head. Simple layout and images, comprehensive information, but not overwhelming. Something for moms
on every stage of the journey as they make their way through.
And around. And back. Because a healthy mom has the power
to change things—the power of moms is real. Especially when
we unite.

*We are a sisterhood. A club. A flock. We are moms who love
a child suffering with the disease of addiction, and together
we are a mighty force. I never would have wanted to be a
part of this group, but now that I am, I'm immensely grateful for the love and support. Bonded in spirit, we are carried
forward, onward, and upward on the wings of one another's
strengths.*

Bonded by heartache and a tormented maternal love, we've known each other forever—even if we've never met. Don't ruffle our feathers—our defensive instincts are strong; together we take care of all the other moms. We validate. We protect. We take the frightened and the fallen under our wings, keeping them safe until they are able to brave the storm. We understand feelings of utter failure (even though, failures we are not). We are the moms of addicts. And we are not alone.

There is strength and power in numbers. Uplifted by one another, we're like a gaggle of amazing geese.

—Tending Dandelions, 232

I, we, have wings.

You have roots to remind you where you're from,
and wings to show you what you can become.

—UNKNOWN

8

Becoming

Perhaps the butterfly is proof that you can go through a great deal of darkness yet become something beautiful.

—BEAU TAPLIN

Dear Self,

Only you will be with yourself every single day for the rest of your life. You need to make decisions and take actions just for you and your future—decisions and actions that will leave you whole and happy. You need to do whatever it takes, even if, especially if, doing whatever it takes means taking care of yourself first. Your life and heart may be broken, but they can be mended. You can stop the damage to yourself from getting worse.

Only you will be with yourself every single day for the rest of your life. You need to move forward—seeking vitality and embracing happiness—without guilt. You need to do whatever it takes to feel beautiful, inside and out. Your life and heart may be broken, but you don't need to look and feel ruined. You can start to glow again, from the inside out. You can.

Love,
Yourself

—"Hello, Gorgeous!" *Readings for Moms of Addicts*

First, I was a daughter and a sister, roles that just happened (and rolled along nicely). Then I chose to become a wife and a mom, roles that brought me such happiness and fulfillment until those roles disappeared. And then, for the first time in my life, my primary role wasn't attached to any larger self-identity, and I had no understanding of what it meant to be *just me*. At an age beyond middle age, I didn't know how I would ever find joy, or feel valued, or be complete on my own—but, having walked this path for a while now (and, to be honest, sometimes having barely crawled), I know that those things are (and always have been) an inside job.

And so, I am *becoming*.

I have been a long time in the making. From kid to sort-of-an-adult to wife to mom. To this new me on the solo flight I'm now on. A *me* I'm still trying to figure out. And become. I'm not the *me* I thought I would be at this age—I thought I'd still be rolling along in a different role altogether—but the inner *me* is much the same *me* as it's been since forever. A *me* that needs purpose— meaningful, making-the-world-a-little-better, hands-and-heart-on-connections-with-other-people purpose.

To be honest, that *me* was buried pretty deep when I first headed off to college in pursuit of a degree in interior design and fun parties, but, while talented at both, it didn't take long for me to figure out that neither was something I wanted to do for the rest of my life. It didn't take long for me to feel purposelessness in my direction. Eventually, following a long night of tearful introspection, I made the decision to join the Peace Corps—but, as it turned out, at nineteen I was too young and inexperienced to join the folks doing good work overseas. Not giving up, I found a national volunteer organization instead, one that connected me with an elementary school in the Appalachian Mountains that needed an assistant for their first-grade teacher for a year. With zero background and lots of enthusiasm, off I went, ready to help someone help a bunch of little someones to learn.

Enchanted with West Virginia from the moment Sister Clare picked me up from the airport, I quickly settled in to the little coal-mining town near the winding Monongahela River. My home for the year was a convent where I lived dormitory-style with a small group of nuns, a couple of other volunteers, a beagle, and a snuffly, snorty bulldog. We ate our meals together around a few tables in the dining room and watched *Fantasy Island* and the news in the evenings; after we got to know each other a bit, a couple of the traditional-habit-wearing nuns even helped me to choose a cute dress for a hot date.

The red brick elementary school was down the hill from the convent, just a short walk on a curving path. There was one teacher (or less) for each grade, and the first-grade class where I was to help out had about thirty kids. Even with so many little desks lined up in rows and two reading tables at the back, the classroom was spacious, with wall-to-wall windows on two sides, looking out over an expanse of ever-color-changing treetops. Before the school year began, I helped the first-grade teacher, Sister Mary Ann, get the classroom ready—decorating bulletin boards, arranging tiny chairs, and putting students' names in books—but age and illness made it impossible for her to continue. After a couple of weeks, I was handed the reins, and I taught first grade for the rest of the year on my own. A job that was an unexpectedly perfect fit.

I loved everything about being a teacher. I loved planning lessons and activities that the kids would enjoy. I loved greeting the passel of six- and seven-year-olds as they came scampering into the classroom every morning, bubbling over with smiles and hugs. And I loved helping them to figure out how to read and spell words, how to add and subtract numbers, how to speak up but speak softly, and how to get along. I loved leading the eager little sponges in my care to the discovery that learning is fun. And I loved doing something that made a difference every single day—a difference I could see. A difference that mattered. When I returned to college the next fall, it was with real purpose, having discovered the wonders of a career that I had never before even considered.

While I lived with the nuns, they taught me how to pray a *novena,* a prayer recited faithfully over nine days, and I tried it out by praying really hard for the health and happiness of my future husband and kids—a husband and kids that I did not yet know, but I hoped I'd someday have—hoping to protect them from all things bad in advance. Years later, Josh, then Joey, then Rick came into my life, the husband and kids I'd been blindly sending up prayers for, each one of them more wonderful than I had hoped or imagined. My most important job became *family,* giving me a purpose more important than any other. The giving and receiving of love and patience, care and trust, and a whole bunch of life lessons.

> *Life before children was like singing a song without knowing the words, or like knowing soft without having touched a puppy's forehead. My days were far less full-bodied then, but I didn't realize that until I had Joey and Rick. A first-grade teacher before my children were born, I have had the full-time job of "Mom" ever since. I wanted to be home to catch a glimpse of the unexpected precious moments—and to put a halt to the not-so-precious ones, too. Because our family moved on to a new state or country with near-biannual rhythm, there seemed to be a constant need for beds, balls, bodies, and beginnings to be hustled along and settled in. My boys have brought out the best in me and the worst in*

*me—they've brought out all of me—and I'm more the person
I was meant to be for having been their mom.*

—The Joey Song, 5

As Joey and Rick grew older, more independent, my most mean-ingful *making-the-world-a-little-better, hands-and-heart-on-connections-with-other-people* purpose became less hands-on, so I had time to add some new layers, starting in India when our family moved there. The poverty was everywhere, all the time, and I knew right away that I needed to do something to make a difference—the only other alternative was *indifference,* and I couldn't live with that for the next two years.

Within the first few weeks, I met my like-minded and soon-to-be cohort and friend, Cindy, at an American Women's Association meeting at the United States embassy, right across the street from where Josh, the boys, and I lived. We started out visiting orphan-ages to hug and feed babies—*so many* mom-less babies, mostly baby girls—which quickly evolved into so much more. Together, Cindy and I founded Moms' Circle of Love, welcoming the big hearts of other moms wanting to help us on our mission: "*The abundance of blessings that have graced our lives are now being re-alized and cherished with new understanding, and we want to share some of what we've been given. Together we can make a difference, one little life at a time.*"

Babies arrived at the orphanages anonymously, via a basket placed outside the front door (with a bell to announce the de-livery), or in batches from far-flung places, often in disturbing condition—malnourished and with tuberculosis, scabies, or more serious afflictions, seriously affecting their chances at life or of ever being adopted. Like baby Zahira. When I first met her, she was lying on her back, bent such that her feet could comfort the sides of her face, rocking from side to side, slowly. A tiny little thing with sticklike arms and legs and an unbelievably distended stomach, she appeared to be about three or four months old until she lit up my world with a big, toothy smile when I picked her up. Zahira was actually eighteen months old, and she couldn't sit, crawl, or stand because she'd been born with a rectum that wasn't hooked up quite right and only the tiniest opening through which to pass waste, so she had been suffering with the consequences of that her entire life.

When the nuns asked Cindy and me if we could find a doctor to help Zahira, we soon discovered she weighed only twelve pounds, had a colon the size of an adult's that was compressing her little lungs, and would need a colostomy followed by numerous reconstructive surgeries. Working with local doctors and hospitals, we were able to get everything done, nursing Zahira to health both before and after her procedures in the comfort and warmth of our homes and families. Eventually, we returned a walking, talking, and digesting Zahira back to the orphanage, and soon she was adopted by a lovely couple from Australia. Four more times, the nuns asked us to help another baby in critical condition, and four more times we did.

Most days of the week, while our kids were in school, Cindy and I helped out a handful of orphanages any way we could. When we noticed the diapers the babies and toddlers wore—a bandanna-weight triangle wrapped around-and-about and then knotted in front—leaked, making slippery puddles on the hard floors—dangerous for everyone, but most especially the barefoot new little walkers—Moms' Circle of Love replaced the thin fabric with thick cloth diapers and plastic covers. When we noticed rows of babies lying in cribs for long hours with no stimulation, we designed crib activity panels to attach to the sides—

buying the colorful fabrics and unbreakable mirrors and rattles and squeakers—and then finding someone to make them (there was nowhere to buy such a thing). Oh, the excitement when we hung them all up! When we noticed that the metal cribs had peeling paint, we recruited the Boy Scouts to repaint them. When one too many toddlers clonked their head on the cold, hard floors, we bought huge, wide rolls of Styrofoam and brown vinyl, enough to cover the room where the toddlers played, and Joey glued it all together to make cushy, waterproof, wall-to-wall floor mats. We raised money for surgeries, provided books and toys and swamp coolers, and took Christmas dinner to the nuns, with all the fixings. Moms' Circle of Love had lots of mom volunteers and lots of support.

But we could only do so much.

Sometimes we would see things that broke our hearts. Like when a caregiver would sit on the floor—propped against the wall with a baby lying on its back between her outstretched legs—pouring scalding-hot spoonfuls of porridge into a little mouth that still needed to suck. Or when we would arrive to find four or five babies lying together in a crib draped with a sheet, all crimson and sweaty from hot steam pumping in, a treatment to clear their lungs. Or when a soon-to-be-adopted baby fell out of a crib onto the hard floor, landing on her head, never to be quite right (and her pending adoption canceled), because someone put her in a crib meant for newborns, not standers. The moms of Moms' Circle of Love did what we could, modeling for the caregivers how to hold and feed the babies, how to play and interact with the babies, how to do things in ways that were safe. And we were a regular part of the babies' lives at an impressionable time when they needed to feel loving attachment. Even if nothing we did endured once we moved back to the United States, what we did mattered while we were there. It mattered in the moment. In the moment of each baby's life.

There were so many things we couldn't change; we were only visitors, after all. (However, to be honest, we did try to change pretty much everything but realized we had to reel things back if we were to remain welcomed.) It was frustrating and painful, but eventually we changed the things we could and *made the best of that.* This is a life lesson I've revisited over and over and over ever since. It was in the orphanages of India that I first figured this out—the one thing I have control over is how I handle things, no matter how much I wish I could control something more—but it has been true with Joey's addiction, with my aging parents, with my divorce, and with growing old on my own. As it says in the Serenity Prayer,

> *God, grant me the serenity*
> *to accept the things I cannot change,*
> *courage to change the things I can,*
> *and wisdom to know the difference.*

These words were my guide when I started the program cooking with the young men at the group home, and later when I started cooking with the young girls at the maternity home, too. These words helped me to remember that my influence is both limited and unlimited; limited in scope, but unlimited in value if I keep my heart wide open and my ego set aside. So, week after week, I just kept showing up, my goals being good food, flexibility, and fun, while cooking and sharing a meal with some other moms' children. Simple as that. It's the moments that matter, the small things we do when the big things are out of our control. This is where the magic happens. Where heartache meets healing. Where love takes wing. (Like the Butterfly Effect):

It has been said that something as small as the
flutter of a butterfly's wings can ultimately cause
a typhoon halfway around the world.

—Unknown

Oh, the power of butterfly wings.

I *believe.*

Now that I'm looking, I see a lifelong pattern that makes clear what's important to me, of which my writing and helping other moms with addicted children is the newest thread. I need to be true to my *purpose*—I need to continue pursuing the things that come naturally and that fill my soul—in my search for a late-in-life career. I want to be a success, but also, and more importantly, I want to be of *value.* Now that I've made the move to Minnesota, the big brave move to start the big brave life, I need to take a leap of faith. I need to do what is meaningful to me. And I need to find the courage to fly.

My hands may be tied, but that doesn't mean I can't un-
leash the protective fury that addiction has wrought. I may
hate The Addict, but I love My Child, and everything I do
can still reflect that. I may be hobbled, but I am fierce.

I will channel my need to do something for my child into
something that means *something. For* him. *Even if he's no-*
where around. I will put my energies into doing something
with real heft and might.

I will use my power wisely: I will not *do something just for*
the sake of doing something. I will not *do something just be-*
cause it makes me *feel good, when it actually might hurt the*
son that I love. I will not *do something for him when doing*
nothing might be the better way to go.

Instead, I will speak out about addiction. This is something
I can do for my son without hurting him. My direct influence
on him may be restricted, but I'm not completely bound and
gagged. For my son, I will educate anyone who will listen.
I will defend the truth. I will open eyes and hearts and minds.

—*Tending Dandelions,* 220

I am *becoming* (although, I realize now, I have been *becoming* all along).

I wish things were different. I wish Josh hadn't taken the middle of my life, leaving only the ends behind like two crusts lying amid crumbs from a loaf of bread. I wish addiction hadn't grabbed hold of Joey, convulsing his world and mine with fears and tears for more than half his life. I wish a long string of circumstances, all out of Rick's control, hadn't caused him to lose so much. And I wish Mom and Dad hadn't slipped down the slope of dementia, losing a bit more of who they once were with each passing day. *I wish I were part of one big happy and healthy family, still able to be connected and tuned in and in touch*—but I'm not. And no matter how hard I wish my wishes, wishing for things to be different isn't going to change a thing. I cannot get stuck in that place. *Wishing.* I don't know what lies ahead—things keep happening, my life and the people in it continue to change and evolve, and things may or may not turn out okay. But I will do the hard work required to ensure that *I* will be okay no matter what.

It's up to me to become my own hero.

It's up to me to collect my heartache and wishes and turn them into something good.

Just a few days ago, it snowed. In May. But even with winter worming its way into spring—following months of arctic temps and mountains of snow—winter in Minnesota hasn't been as bad as I'd imagined; for probably the first (and last) time in my life, a buildup of worry and overthinking worked to my advantage. Looking out my window as I sit at my desk this morning, it looks like spring has finally triumphed—Mother's Day is warm and sunny with green buds on the trees and tulips blooming in gardens up and down the street. (Since I moved into my house midwinter, I won't have trees or grass or flowers in my own yard for a while). Sipping on a cup of hot coffee, I open my laptop and navigate to the new MomPower website. Two months in the making, today it is live, launching in support of moms with addicted children on one of the most difficult holidays of the year:

As moms living in the place where love and addiction meet, our hearts are always confused and hurting—but as Mother's Day nears, our tender hearts seem to become even more so. As moms with addicted children, this day doesn't feel or look the way it's supposed to. I realize it's just a manufactured holiday, but still, it hurts not being loved and appreciated on the "official day" of maternal love and appreciation. But, we can find strength and comfort in each other—and in the enduring blessing that is motherhood—*and we can celebrate* that: *the realities, the hurt, and the blessings of motherhood, which, hopefully, collectively, bring some peace to your heart.*

As moms with addicted children, we grieve that our lives didn't turn out the way we imagined; we ache that we aren't able to protect our children the way we were meant to; and we often feel like our love is a failure—even though the truth is that if a mother's love could fix addiction, it would, long ago, have been eradicated.

Still, a mother's love is mighty.

We can draw strength and comfort from one another, and we can re-learn how to treasure the treasures, knowing that great love comes with great pain—it's just part of the deal.

I will always be a mother—I was given two precious miracles, one to hold in each hand—and nothing can ever take away the splendor of that. That splendor is ours, each of ours, to hold on to, to treasure, forever.

The arrival of Mother's Day may bring great sadness, but there are also blessings to be celebrated. No matter what happens—or doesn't happen—this Mother's Day, I will remember that this special day isn't just about soaking up the love and appreciation of my children; *it's just as much about reveling in the blessings of* being *a mother—the gifts.*

MomPower takes flight.

When designing the concept, the feel, of MomPower, I chose a simple butterfly as our *mom with an addicted child* symbol—an elegant purple stroke with wings like a heart—because no matter where life takes our children, a mom's love always follows. The flutter of which carries great power. In bringing MomPower to life, in creating a community of voices and support for moms with addicted children, I've found healing within myself, too. I may not be able to help Joey directly, but I believe that someday, some way, my love and hope and help will land on his shoulders, carried on the wings of other moms—I believe the love and help and hope of all of us, together, comes full circle with *healing.* By moms and for moms, MomPower is a place for the healing to begin.

I visit Mom on her special day, bringing a Mother's Day headband with pink-winged yellow bumblebees bobbling about, and it's just as big a hit as the last one. After our parade through the hall, bringing joy to both Mom and the other residents, Mom dismisses me with a subtle-but-not-so-subtle "You look tired; do you need a nap?" Her polite way of getting rid of visitors when she's had enough. I bring Dad back to my house for the day; Mom has never come here and never will. She hasn't left her building or been in a car for years (except for the time she went to the hospital in an ambulance), so coaxing her into coming here would likely result in a halfway-down-the-highway panicked disaster. Instead, I take lots of pictures so she *feels* like she's been here and to help her understand that I'm in Minnesota for good. After Dad and I eat a light lunch, we clear the dishes from the dining table and spread out some leftover packing paper so we can fix an antique spinning wheel that was broken to bits in the move. He likes to help and to fix stuff, so I've been saving projects for him that he's still able to do. We go down into the basement and rummage through the workbench drawers for the bottle of wood glue, a mallet, a file, and some shims, and then we spend the afternoon working on putting the spinning wheel back together. Dad calls me *Mom* a few times; it just casually slips out, not at all sarcastically, like the times when he's called me *Mom* before.

I've been working on projects around my new house on my own, too. Like hanging a heavy wooden valance over the sliding doors in the dining room—using two ladders, my shoulders, and (since I have no muscles in my arms) sheer will. And like setting up my speakers and smart lightbulbs, orchestrating the lights and music or news to turn on and off throughout my house at perfectly timed intervals. I'm determined to figure things out and get things done (and done right). But still, I have to move to a different TV if I accidentally bump a wrong button on the remote. And then there was the situation with the enormous weighted umbrella on my deck—I attached it to the railing with a bungee cord and left it open to see how well my handiwork worked in a light wind.

It blew over the railing and was left hanging upside down, ten feet wide and wide open, the top (now the bottom) dangling about a foot above the mud that is still my yard. Another whole situation to figure out. But I did.

Over the years, I've discovered all sorts of things that I'm good at and plenty of things that I'm not—but either way, I keep trying out new things and don't easily give up, just as I've been doing with all the makings of my new life. I've figured out how to write books and get published—although, I must admit, I've never figured out how to type with more than two fingers. And I've never figured out how to parallel park. But I have figured out how to do my own marketing, build my own website, speak in front of large audiences, and redirect (and reinvent) my direction more than a few times—all through a loose system of trial and error and a lot of talking (and some cussing) to myself. I am capable. I am moving forward.

Until I'm not.

Suspended in midair and waiting to fall, I'm mad at myself for how vulnerable and insecure I feel when there's another tug on my rug.

Me: *Alimony was due yesterday. Whenever you're making holiday plans, please also plan to fulfill your obligation before—rather than after—the first of each month. My mortgage, health insurance, and other major bills are due on the first, which don't get paid when you leave me hanging. You've taken everything else; don't cause me to lose my house and credit, too.*

Josh replies—a preemptive rug ripple: *I continue to try and maintain and grow my business but am concerned that I will see a slow-down in the next twelve months due to economic indicators. That is stated only as an FYI to you versus any other message.*

My *becoming* becomes undone.

Wherever, however I regroup, replant, and rebuild, it seems

I can't count on Josh to stop shaking the foundation on which I stand. I wish he were still the reliable person I once knew, the person he was when he was my other half for half my life. I wish my shared history with Josh—as friends and lovers and parents—meant that my financial security would feel more like a promise, or indebtedness, or even *duty* to him than a burden or an annoyance to be dismissed with a flick of the wrist. I wish Josh had meant the vow he made when we got married (and again when we got divorced)—that I'd never have to worry about my future because he'd always be the guy that *did right.* I wish I had an employment history to lean on so I could rely on only *myself* to support myself. And I wish—oh, how I wish—that Josh's actions (and inactions) didn't have the power to make me feel worthless over and over and over again, which makes being alone even harder than it sometimes is anyway (and harder than it needs to be). But here I go again, *wishing,* even though I know wishing isn't going to change what *is* to what *should be.* I can't control what Josh (or anyone else) does or doesn't do. I can only control how I respond to whatever life hands out.

I can collect my heartache and wishes and turn them into something good.

There isn't anything easy about accepting hard truths that I don't want to be true—like having become *something less than nothing* to Josh. Or anything else in life that has been too horrible to want to comprehend. But *acceptance* is the beginning of *healing.* It means pulling my head out of the sand, facing reality, and taking it *head-on* instead of relying on wishful thinking and being devastated by relentless unsurprising surprises. Realize. Accept. Deal. Acceptance is the beginning of moving forward in a healthy way, of taking back some sort of control. As I learned with Joey and his addiction, acceptance is *Step One.*

Begrudging acceptance: This is where I am now. It took a long time to get here; I really fought it. How could I possibly accept *this horrendous thing that has obliterated my child and my life? How could I* accept *that my child is an addict? How could I* accept *the fact that I no longer even know how to be my child's mom? The family is broken, the dream is dead, my son is suffering, and I can't help him. I'm suffering and no one can help me. There have been too many trage-dies to* accept *any part of this. Too much agony. Too much unfairness. Too much wrong.* Accept? *Resign myself? Give the stamp of approval? Put out a welcome mat? I think not.*

But acceptance *of my son's addiction doesn't mean any of those things. It doesn't mean I am emotionally rolling over, giving consent, or submitting to the beast. Acceptance means that I* recognize the truth. *And I do—but I don't like it. Maybe someday I'll get to* full-fledged acceptance. *But for now, I'm at begrudging acceptance:* It is what it is. *Addiction has changed things from the way they were meant to be.*

—*Tending Dandelions*, 93

Sigh. Life has changed *so many* things from the way they were meant to be. And the forces of life and love and loss sometimes feel overwhelming.

It's just a matter of time until Dad will need to be moved from assisted living to memory care. We have him on the waiting list, so he'll have a space when the time comes. But everyone involved is trying to hold off as long as possible, until Dad is beyond the point where he'd surely spend his days banging on the locked doors try-ing to get out. Dad is social and active and needs to be free—he's able to manage his established routine on his own for the most part, all neat and tidy, even if his short-term memory is rapidly fading—and we all agree that moving him too soon would probably, literally, kill him. But there are risks. Dad loves to walk outside every day—but what if he gets lost? Or crosses the street at the wrong time? Or can't find the piece of paper in his wallet with the code to get back into the building? Risks. Big risks. We can only hope we're making the right decision when balancing safety versus happiness and freedom versus jail along with the rest of Dad's life.

The situation is so different with Mom. She is snug and content within the confines of her little world, accepting bribes of Hershey's Kisses in order for bath time to happen and refusing to wear anything besides her favorite pajamas. I've come to picture dementia sort of like Swiss cheese, with everyone's slice being very different—random holes in different places, with different capabilities falling into the holes and leaving different capabilities behind, over different spans of time—and Mom's and Dad's slices of Swiss cheese are opposites. Before, I had thought of dementia more like a *sauce reduction*—condensing everyone's personality to its utmost essence—but that doesn't seem to be the case. If it were, Mom would be a sweet swirl of pure sugar, kind and gentle and polite. Instead, Mom has become bossy and crabby with Dad over the past several years, and since he no longer hears very well, the things she is bossy and crabby at him about go right over his head, making Mom even more bossy and crabby, leaving Dad hurt and confused during his many daily visits. Visits to straighten her bed, fill her glass of water, and make sure she's okay.

It's hard to watch this end-of-life dynamic that's so different from the one they shared pre-dementia—and it's a dynamic we need to keep in mind when the time comes to move Dad to memory care; it's obvious that Mom and Dad shouldn't live in the same apartment together—that would be way too much togetherness, a togetherness that would be toxic. But what's *not* clear is if the long-married bride and groom should live in the same wing or on very separate floors. Thank goodness we don't have to decide yet, but none of us knows whether *togetherness* or *apartness* would do the least damage. Always, it seems, life presents a nesting doll set of impossible conundrums.

> *In leaving India with one son, I leave the other behind. That there's no real choice in my doing so doesn't make this any easier. Even though Rick will be in the caring hands of my friend Cindy and her family until Josh's solo return, I'm leaving him parentless in a foreign country. I feel sick not knowing when I'll see him again. Dropping him off at his temporary home, I walk Rick to the front door. He's ready to make a quick good-bye of this, but I don't care. I take a deep breath and freeze the moment. Closing my eyes, I inhale the aroma of chocolate mixed with boy sweat, and I memorize the feel of barely-there bristles rubbing against my cheek as I hold my young son close.*

> —*The Joey Song,* 7

Every day is Groundhog Day, with Mom and Dad's dysfunctional patterns now stuck on repeat, but also, every day is a new day, and every visit is a new visit; neither of them remember whatever happened last. They're simply carried forward into the next moment, powered by their love and past. Mom still tells stories about how she and Dad would go skating or take long walks back when they were dating because they didn't have money to do anything else, adding how perfect those dates were and how lucky she is to have married such a good man. Dad still tells about walking up the aisle as husband and wife, gazing at Mom as he says how beautiful she was then, and how beautiful she looks now—not seeing her disheveled hair and missing teeth. *To have and to hold, till death do us part.*

I wish I had that. That missing ingredient in my life of being single—to be someone's number one. To be the person someone would want to check on first when someday the earth shakes. But that's not going to happen. By choice now, at this point. I'm a one-family woman; it feels like it would be a betrayal somehow (why or to whom, I'm not sure) to start up a different family by adding someone else's family to the one I already started.

I need to collect my heartache and wishes and turn them into something good.

There's a bird's nest tucked among the faux violets and berries of the wreath hanging on my front door. For days, a mama bird was flying back and forth, carrying tiny twigs and tucking them into place, getting her nest set up just right, some sort of finch, I think. Then, one day, she was sitting on five speckled blue eggs, protecting them and keeping them warm until they hatched. Before long, Mama Bird was busy doing what she needed to do to keep her babies alive—finding food and feeding them well so that one day soon they'd be ready to fly. And then, yesterday, when I walked out through the garage and around to the porch to take another peek, the nest was empty. Just some feathers strewn about on the welcome mat and the cement of the porch floor. Everyone Mama Bird had been devoting her life to was gone. Did the babies grow up and fly away the way nature intended? Or did something devastating happen? Something that plucked the babies from the family nest before their time? The mom still comes around; I can see her out my desk window as she swoops in and out. Checking. I wonder if she feels like I do—*What happened? Was I a failure as a mother? As the keeper of the family? And what do I do now?*

For ten years now, I've spent most evenings alone—about 3,650 dinners. There are benefits to this, for sure; I can cook what I want, I can make a meal out of just popcorn if I feel like it, and there aren't many dishes to wash. Living alone means I don't have to pick up anyone else's socks or bicker about how the dishwasher is loaded (or not), or worry because someone is late when the roads are icy. But it also means a sparseness of closeness, and a struggle to fall and stay asleep. And saying *good morning* to only Alexa.

An empty nest feels very empty. An empty nest hurts. But *feeling* the empty feelings—acknowledging them instead of stuffing them down—is what makes filling the emptiness with goodness possible. (Eventually.) Really. So, I'm *feeling*. With care.

> *My heart is fragile. My spirit is fragile. They're like threads of spun sugar; I need to handle them with care. I need to put soft gloves on the thoughts and feelings that might break me. I need to be gentle with myself.*
>
> *All day, every day, I carry around sharp-edged emotions that are as much a part of me as the lines they have carved on my face. But every time such emotions give me a nudge, I don't need to respond by giving them a close look. And I don't need to grab them by fistfuls or armloads or boatloads, setting myself up to become overwhelmed. I can take out each thought and feeling, one by one, on an as-needed basis, give it the time and attention it needs, then put it back, very carefully, like a knife in a drawer.*
>
> *I know the damage that can be done by feeling too fully the things that have hurt me. My heart is fragile. My spirit is fragile. I need to handle them gingerly, gently, softly.*
>
> —Tending Dandelions, 143

I'm feeling grief over the loss of my family, of my marriage, and of Joey and Mom and Dad while they're still alive. A bunch of big deaths without bodies.

And I'm feeling afraid. Not of dying, but of dying alone—literally, actually *dying* alone.

I'm feeling sad that the comforts usually given freely during times of great loss—like flowers and casseroles and circling wagons—are stifled by stigma, or by simply *not knowing what to say or do,* or by the lack of tidy closure. I wish people understood that loss is loss, whether a marriage is brought to an end by an unexpected divorce or by a death, and that heartache is heartache, whether a child suffers with the disease of addiction or with any other disease.

Years ago, I shared with Joey what it felt like from *my* side of his addiction. Today, everything—my divorce and broken family and my parents' dementia—sort of feels the same way. Everything that has happened, all of it, has broken hearts and bonds and all the rules:

> *Unlike the disease of addiction, cancer doesn't destroy the love in relationships. With addiction, I sit empty-handed watching you kill yourself. With addiction we each walk through hell alone.*
>
> —*The Joey Song,* 194

I feel overcome with *bittersweetness* when looking at photos—Josh and me standing at the altar with our 1980s hair, Joey and Rick blowing out birthday candles or playing in the yard, Mom and Dad doing mom-and-dad stuff over the years—moments that were, at the time, wrapped in an invisible cloak of love and the eternalness of togetherness. Moments, memories, now all smudged by devastation of one sort or another. An internal lifeline to hang on to, lost.

I *feel.* But sometimes I don't feel at all. Or, to be more accurate, I don't *allow* myself to feel; I eat my feelings instead. And then I feel rather *unbecoming*. Like when I loop a rubber band around the button and buttonhole on the waist of my jeans for a little extra room when getting dressed in the morning. Or when I add another cute shirt to the growing pile of clothes that no longer fit, hidden away on the top shelf in my closet. Some people might think (judge) I've *let myself go* (in the midst of letting go of so much). But it's not on purpose—I mean, it's not that I've just *given up*. Rather, *eating* has become a friend for me to hang out with in the evenings while watching TV. In place of being held and heard. This is not the healthiest adaptive behavior, I know. But still, little by little, *I am becoming*.

Becoming, you see, is not *perfection*. It's not pain-free. And it's not a straight line—it's a back-and-forth, up-and-down process, held together by rubber bands and who knows what else. It is not *done and done*. It's messy and it's hard work. But it is *living*.

Becoming means collecting my heartache and wishes and turning them into something good.

Some days, I become overwhelmed with the wrongness of everything. With not understanding what has happened. Or how or why. Some days, I allow myself to think of all the worst things that have happened and that might still happen. And, I allow myself to think that things will never, ever get better. Some days, I just have to wallow around for a while.

Then, when I'm done being morose, I remember that things will never, ever get better if I don't help them along. I remember that things getting better grows from the inside out. What blooms is what was planted; my tomorrow starts with that.

Some days, I need to work extra hard on my inner serenity—knowing there's such healing power in that. I need to remind

myself to keep my heart open to trust and hope and honesty.
I remind myself that happy memories, peaceful memories,
like flowers in a garden, are beautiful gifts. So I collect those
memories and let them gently tickle my mind. And I remind
myself to fill my thoughts, my world, with happy things, not
sad things; right things, not wrong things.

Whatever is good. I remind myself, daily, to grow that.

—Tending Dandelions, 214

Inside and out, I will be—*I am*—the mistress of my domain. I alone am responsible for what I say and do (or don't do), how hard I try (or don't try), what I think, and what I do with those thoughts. I alone own my mistakes and whether I learn from them. And I own the consequences of all of that—good or bad. (But I'm *not* responsible for and cannot control any of that for anyone else, *period*—even though I sometimes think I am and think I can—which is freeing.) The consequences of someone else's behavior might come knocking, but I alone control the level of love, peace, and positive energy entering my world. Just because something hateful, disturbing, or negative is at the gate doesn't mean I have to let it into my psyche and heart. I need to take care of myself because I *deserve* to be well taken care of, first and foremost, but also because I'm no good to anyone else if I don't. *You can't pour from an empty cup.* No one can do my *becoming* for me. (Just as I can't do the work of *becoming* for anyone else. Urrgh.)

Listening to my instincts and following my principles—living with integrity and as much grace and humor as I can muster—*I am* up to *me.*

I've learned a few things about making things better rather than worse over the years. Usually the hard way—either from the mistakes I've made or from crawling my way out of piles of crap into which I've been tossed. Rarely have I learned anything simply because I was *told* how to do it, and I don't always do what I've learned (or apply what I know)—even though I know I should, *for my own sake,* for goodness sake. But, I persevere, pulling myself up by my bootstraps, and try not to beat myself up when I didn't do what needs doing and need to get started all over again. (Which is often.) And I try not to be afraid.

Negative self-talk (that evil inner whisperer) must be silenced—the one that says I'm not good enough or capable enough. And the negative talk from *the powers that wanna be* must be silenced, too. I'm the one who knows my strengths, abilities, and limitations best. I'm the one who knows the things I'm good at that also make me feel good. *I'm* the one who needs to believe in me.

It's okay to be happy, even when I hurt—and even when the people I love hurt, too. It's okay to embrace the things that make me happy, to have fun (without guilt). And it's okay *not to be okay*—some days finding happiness is just too much work. Feelings of fun and joy ebb and flow, just like feelings of pain and loss ebb and flow, too. It's okay to *fake it till you make it*—sometimes a smile comes from joy, but sometimes joy can be found in cracking a smile. And sometimes saying "I'm *just dandy*" helps being *just dandy* become true. So does talking more about the *good* things in life than the bad.

Be a voice, not an echo.

Believe.

Embracing the *now*—not getting stuck in the past or being consumed by the worries of tomorrow—changes everything. Being one with *what is.* Acceptance. Acknowledging what I miss while appreciating what I have. Today.

Notes to self, in no particular order: Make goals. Have reasonable expectations. Let go of perfection and practice forgiveness—

for myself and for others. And let go of this destructive trio: shame, blame, and guilt. Hug often. Don't get stuck in the weeds; keep the big picture in sight for both sanity and perspective. Be a good friend. Talk and talk and talk isn't a substitute for *accept* and *do.* There are no magical solutions. No snarkiness, ever. Getting dressed and brushing my hair every day is essential in avoiding a downward spiral. It's hard enough to change myself—it's impossible to change other people. Maintain healthy boundaries. Being nice doesn't mean being a doormat. Try walking in someone else's shoes at least once a day. Purposeful action (or inaction) is better than *reaction*; be prepared. Be mindful of mountains and molehills: life is full of chaos and trauma, bad things that *just happen*—don't be (or be with) someone who *makes* that sort of stuff happen. And, lastly, every bit of heartache can be turned into something good by helping someone else who's hurting.

By collecting my heartache and wishes and turning them into something good, I am *becoming* the best me possible. I am *becoming* from the inside out.

In *The Four Agreements* by Don Miguel Ruiz, I've found an inspirational guide. I will put his words into practice, taking care to be impeccable with my word—speaking with integrity, saying what I mean, and using the power of my words for truth and love. I will do my best in all circumstances—considering my capabilities at any particular moment. I will make every effort to *not* take things personally, letting the opinions and actions of others roll right on by without crushing me, without turning me into a victim. And I will not make assumptions; instead, I will ask questions and communicate clearly in order to avoid drama and trauma.

Such wise and simple rules I will internalize to help keep my *becoming* on track.

One by one and one after another, different threads have woven their way through my heart and life—all the heartache and wishes, all the things I've learned and all the things I wish I haven't had to learn. Addiction, then divorce, then dementia. And all the good things I've been given, like Rick, my family when we were a family, and love. So many threads. Woven among the threads that were already there but tucked out of sight was a me I hadn't been totally aware of. A strength I didn't know I had. All the threads, woven together, in and out and up and around over the years, create the fabric of my life, a tapestry. And I am the artist; the best me I can be is in my own hands.

Sometimes people say things like, "It will all turn out fine." Well, no, it very well might not. Sometimes, many times, things are out of my control and *it* will only turn out fine if I do the work to make it fine inside my own head and heart. And sometimes I hear, "God won't give you more than you can handle." Well, a quick look at the statistics for substance abuse and suicide shows that adage isn't true, either. The threads of pain and suffering are *real*.

I may still look like the cuddly old mom I once was, but like silk, I'm strong as steel. I've been forged from the fire I thought would kill me.

I've heard people say—both addicts and their parents, once they made it through the hell of addiction—that they're grateful for the journey. That they're better people because of the fiery trail they were forced to walk.

I hope to be grateful, too, someday, but I'm definitely not grateful yet—grateful might be an overzealous aspiration for someone whose child is still caught in addiction's tight-fisted grip. Addiction has devastated me and my child—my whole family—and there's no end in sight. I am, however, a better person because of it.

I'm more compassionate now. More patient. More tolerant and empathetic. I'm less dramatic. Less judgmental. Less trivial. I've learned and grown in ways I never could have imagined—and didn't really want to imagine.

Through the unwinding of time and elements, I've been completely changed, through and through, like a piece of petrified wood—from sapling to stone. I can never change back to the person I was before all hell broke loose. But that's okay. I'm now solid and strong. I'm a weary, but wise, old relic.

—*Tending Dandelions,* 181

•

As autumn rolls its way out, making room for winter, most of the leaves have fallen to the ground, although a few trees still have some red and yellow hangers-on. I won't have to rake for many years since my four recently planted trees are quite small, but I find other ways to putter around in the yard, like trimming back the coneflowers I planted in my new garden a few months ago and opening the spigots before the first freeze. A couple of pheasants strut through my yard each morning and evening, calling out with a full-throated (off-key) crow, and the birds flocking my feeders seem to be eating as much as they can before it snows. I love autumn; it might be my favorite season. The changing leaves, the cute sweaters and boots, and the anticipation of the holidays ahead, even though holidays are hard. Year after year, the traditions keep evolving because *life* keeps evolving, and there are too many empty seats at my holiday tables—but I've come a long way. And so today, on Thanksgiving (and most days these days), I'm collecting my heartache and wishes and trying to turn them into something good. I'm *feeling* the empty feelings—acknowledging them instead of stuffing them down—and making filling the emptiness with goodness possible. I'm *filling*, not *stuffing*.

When my boys were little, they hovered about the kitchen on Thanksgiving morning, eager to get started with stuffing the turkey. We tied on aprons, washed our hands, pushed step stools over to the kitchen counter, and discussed who, exactly, would need to touch the pale and pimply turkey flesh.

Joey dumped bread cubes into a large bowl and Rick stirred in the onions and sage; they took turns scooping stuffing into the hollow center of our holiday bird before it was slathered in oil and popped in the oven. Our home was full of pleasant aromas and anticipation and things to be thankful for.

Norman Rockwell picture-perfect.

But things changed once Joey became addicted.

Thanksgiving became a day stuffed with unspoken disappointment, anger, and fear rather than too much pie and good cheer. Rick, his dad, and I would wait for Joey to show up—or not show up at all—while our turkey and sweet potatoes shriveled away in the oven. Retreating to different parts of the house, we avoided the sad festivities and phony smiles until tradition beckoned us to sit down at the table across from Joey's very empty place. Thankful, I was not.

It has been a dozen years now since Joey even pretended he was coming home for Thanksgiving dinner. (I don't know where he has turkey. Or if he has turkey.) And so many other things have changed, too. I've had time to adjust to Thanksgiving the way it is and stop wishing for the way it should be, but time hasn't taken away the hurt—or the hole where my family should be. I suspect it never will. Instead, over time, I've grown stronger. Over time, I've learned a few things that have helped me to get through and even enjoy the holidays again.

Make room for your feelings and let go of old expectations. I'm now strong enough to face the hurt rather than stuff it away (more often than not), and I'm strong enough to fill the holes in my life and my heart with things that make the day better, not worse. That means facing reality, not trying to re-create what can't be re-created, starting new traditions, and spending quality time with some happy old memories.

There's a lot wrapped up in this big day that rolls around one short day a year. A lot of hopeful hopes, fears, disappointments, and stress—when holiday tradition and expectation meet addiction, it can be madness. But it's possible to look at things differently, to do things differently, especially if everyone involved is recruited to open their eyes and minds. And when the spirit of things leading up to the big day is giving thanks, that spirit is contagious.

Thanksgiving is meant to be a day for gathering together with loved ones and having fun. So simple—and beautiful, if left simple. A performance, it is not. And live up to unrealistic expectations, I will not.

I no longer spend the weeks leading up to Thanksgiving trying to pretend that everything is fine, that addiction hasn't consumed my son (and that life hasn't consumed my whole family), and that I can still pull off a pretend-perfect performance. I no longer stuff down my sadness, putting on the dressing of normal life in the same way I shove myself into my jeans after a big meal—by taking a deep breath, swallowing the pain, and pasting on a smile.

Instead, I plan ahead. I take the time to face my feelings—I take the time to grieve and cry for what was and what isn't—and then, acknowledging the pitfalls I don't want to fall into, I figure out ways to make the holiday work. And one of those ways is to ask for help—from friends, family, a therapist or counselor or support group.

Celebrate those who are at the table and let go of perfection. I have let go of thinking that I'm the only one who can make the day (any day, actually) perfect, for anyone. Or that I can please everyone. Thanksgiving is made all the better with group participation—which means asking for everyone's hands and hearts to be in the right place at the right time. Together we can prepare and adapt to the fact that our addicted loved one (and any other loved one) might not show up (or worse).

But who is *not* at the table shouldn't take up more space than the people who are.

There is no end to the room I have at my table. And in my heart. But both my heart and home have rules. Before the big day, I set my boundaries (and set up escape hatches), knowing that it's possible that not everyone who shows up is going to behave. I can't control the actions of anyone else, but what I can control is me (and even that is no easy task). When I face reality, my actions don't need to be reactions. My boundaries don't need to be rough, they just need to be strong.

Try something different; open your heart to something new. When the holiday hurts, maybe it's time to try something different—something smaller, or bigger, or somewhere new. The meal, the menu, an old family recipe, the way (or the place) that we've always celebrated Thanksgiving . . . the little traditions mean nothing compared to the meaning of the big tradition itself. There was a time when I would spend weeks shopping and chopping, mixing and rolling, cleaning and decorating, for a meal that, for all of its hype, actually took less than thirty minutes to eat (not counting the time spent talking). But I enjoyed all the creative chaos. Until things changed. And then I didn't. I felt a bit guilty at first, serving store-bought pie or stuffing from the deli, but the reality is, *that* isn't what matters. And no one ever noticed—or if they did, they didn't care.

Share your gratitude and give back. Who is at the table is more important than what is on the table (or where the table is). In the holiday hubbub, it's easy to forget what the holiday is really about.

Giving thanks.

So I've learned, having grown in my own recovery, to make every effort to live in the moment. To give thanks for the moment. To give thanks for those around me—those people who matter and who deserve to feel like they matter, no matter what else is going on. I take the time to soak in and appreciate everything I have to be grateful for. Of which there is a lot.

My need to fill the holes in both my heart and my life is big. And I've found that helping others keeps me moving forward. It may be overwhelming to add one more expectation to a day already laden with so much, but giving thanks by showing thanks doesn't have to fall on one particular day in the fall. I've got 364 other days of the year in which to do what my heart needs to do; it helps me to help moms, day by day, in little ways, with my writing and with MomPower.

Accept what is, one day at a time. Yes, I'm finally strong enough to fill the hole in my life where my family should be with things that make the holiday better, not worse. I'm strong enough to face reality—to accept what is—to start new traditions, and to spend time with some happy old memories. Those are mine to keep and enjoy, forever.

Old memories still have the power to bring tears to my eyes, but I'm finally able to treasure my memories for what they are: gifts. I am blessed to have had so many years of such happiness, and not even addiction or divorce can take that away. After everything that has happened, I still have Joey's and Rick's smiles, the sounds of their voices, and the feel of their hugs, no matter how far away they may be. So, in giving thanks, I take the time to remember *what was* before embracing, fully, *what is*. I laugh, I cry. I allow the movies in my mind to fill my soul.

Many years ago, Joey sent me this message:

*Happy Thanksgiving, Mom. Hopefully, someday I'll give
you a reason to be thankful for me. I love you. Thank you
for still loving me.*

No matter what, I have always been thankful for both of my boys—and I'm thankful they both know how much they are loved. Even though neither Joey nor Rick can be here this year, I carry them with me always—the sounds of their voices and the feel of their hugs—no matter how far away they may be. I have so much to be thankful for today.

This is me *filling*, not *stuffing*.

Not *became*.

But *becoming*.

9

A Legacy

Our fingerprints don't fade from the lives we touch.

—JUDY BLUME

HELLO, 2020. A new year, a new decade . . . and new resolutions. This year, I'm not just going to quit eating chocolate or try to lose somewhere in the range of ten to fifty pounds as usual, though. This year my resolutions are going to be wrapped up in one big goal instead of being what are usually, actually, a smattering of wishes. This year I have a plan—my *Just Dandy* (while living with heartache and wishes) plan, which is a conscious effort to keep moving forward in positive ways instead of losing my way in the turmoil of life, as is so easy to do. Every day I will start by speaking a kind word or two to myself (out loud), followed by making a goal to do at least one thing to help me be the best *me* possible, whatever that may be, whatever I feel up to—big or small, personal or out-reaching—on any given day. And I will jot these things down, because jotting things down helps make them real. Then, every night before going to bed, I will read the nice thing I said to myself when I started my day and will cross off my day's goal, feeling good that I did it. I'm pretty sure that these simple steps will help me to be able to say I'm *just dandy* and mean it (more often than not) with each passing day. If you want to follow my *Just Dandy* plan, too, it's outlined in the back of the book on page 239.

Each morning I will begin by looking at my bedraggled reflection in the mirror and saying something like *hey, your eyebrows are looking good!* as I give them a waggle. Or *hey, what a great idea you had during the night!* (Instead of *ugh, look at all those wrinkles* or *ugh, what a dunce.*) Positive-thinking things, even on those days when positive thinking is a stretch. (Even if all I can come up with is *hey, you got out of bed!*) And I will set an objective, maybe going for a brisk walk or calling a friend who's sad. Or maybe paying my bills or painting my toenails or saving the world, or some other inspired thing that somehow betters me just a bit, and then sometime during the day, I will get that thing done. I'm starting this new habit—folding it into my daily routine—with the intentional intention of elevating myself to the best possible me (which is good for me and for everyone else). This effort is the bridge between whatever is behind me and whatever happens next. Every day is an opportunity to be harnessed.

I get one life, and I want to live the best life I can—no matter what is happening around me. So that's what I'm going to do—one day, one step, one choice at a time.

Rick was here for Christmas, his first visit to my new house since it's been completely built. As always, his presence was the best present ever—it's so true that the things that mean the most simply cannot be bought. He left a few days ago, heading back to New York City to ring in the New Year and then back to work. Today I'm putting away the last of the holiday decorations, the sneaky stragglers that I keep finding, like the Peace on Earth hand towel in the powder room and the little elf with bells on his boots perched on top of the grandfather clock. Carrying the last bits and bobs to the storage shelves in the basement, I stand on a step stool to reach the top shelf. Pushing things around, I come across two boxes tied in twine: ornaments I have saved for my boys—

ornaments I had put in their stockings from their first Christmas till our last, ornaments they would excitedly rummage around to find among all the other ornaments and hang on the tree year after year—along with the ornaments they had made with their own little hands. Next to these boxes is Joey's teddy, kind of flopped on its side. Well, not an *original* teddy—a substitute. Joey's teddy was long ago eaten by one of our always-hungry-and-not-too-particular black labs. When I saw this identical twin bear in a shop a few years ago, I had to have it—especially after having accidentally left Rick's beloved blankie behind on a top shelf when Josh and I parted ways and sold our house. I had to have it so I could set it on the shelf with the ornaments, along with other little stuff from the past that I want to pass on to my boys. Things that mean something to me and hopefully to them—even though I don't know if that transfer will ever happen. (I think my heart just squeezed out a tear.)

Heading back upstairs, I settle into a chair in the living room to think about that very big small thing—that desire to pass stuff on to Joey and Rick. *Something that means something.* What I really want to leave behind is something more like *fingerprints* than mere objects, though—I want to leave behind an imprint on their hearts and souls of *something good.* My boys are now men, but still, they're watching—the circle of life and love and learning never ends. The most important thing I can leave them, my most important legacy as a mom, is *what I do* and *who I am.*

> *I have one life to live, which also happens to be the one gift I have to give my children that really matters. How I live, the example I set (if I do it right), is the richest inheritance that I can leave behind. More valuable than heirloom jewels or velvet bags full of gold, it is a gift that can't be lost, spent too quickly, frittered away, or easily forgotten.*

*Courageous, compassionate, honest, loyal, fair. Even when
no one is looking, even if it seems my children aren't paying
any attention (which they often aren't), my legacy is defined
by how I live my life. Whether I want them to or not, my
children absorb my words, actions, and attitudes in dribs
and drabs as we go, or sometimes, much later, in big, eye-
opening floods.*

*I have one life to live, and how I live it happens to be the
one gift I have to give my children that really matters. I will
strive to be the best possible me—an example, like a wild-
flower reaching beyond the shadows toward the sun.*

—"Legacy," *Readings for Moms of Addicts*

When Joey was little, there was a time when I felt pretty cocky
about my skills as a new mom, but once Rick was born, I realized those "skills" had really been just bits of luck strung together
with wishful thinking; my skills, I discovered, would need a lot
of work. So it was with nothing more than love and good intentions that I stumbled through parenthood—rocking my babies to
sleep, kissing their scraped knees, and setting unwelcome limits
for my sometimes testy teens—while hoping I was doing things
kind of right. Hoping I was somehow giving my boys the right
tools and the right foundation for when the time came for them
to head out into the world on their own—a time that snuck up
on me and came far too soon. When Joey graduated from high
school in India, shortly after his release from the hospital in the
United States, seemingly happy and healthy and having left the
great hiccup behind, I wrote him a letter, and then three years
later I wrote a similar letter to Rick. At the time of those momentous occasions, it seemed like my influence on my grown sons
had more or less come to an end—but now I realize that I could

not have been more wrong. Now, of course, I realize that, as their mom, *what I do* and *who I am* will always have an impact. Good or bad. Intentional or not.

Dear Joey/Rick,

Our years together have been too short. When I first held you in my arms, it seemed like you would be mine forever. Now, here you are, ready to build your own life. I am so proud of the man you have become—just as proud of you now as I was on the day you were born. The first time your dimpled little hands reached out for me, I was there. And I've tried to be there when you have reached out (and even when you haven't) ever since.

Over the past 18 years I have learned about you, about life, about myself—and I have loved you more than life itself. I hope I have guided you in the right direction, but maybe there are some things I forgot to say. Or maybe I said the right things, but not often enough. Or maybe I forgot to tell you or show you how important some of those things are. So, even though I will always be there when you reach out (and even when you don't), I need to put everything into words one more time before you go away.

You are special; you are smart, loving, thoughtful, principled, and devoted; you are a leader and a hard worker. Use these gifts God has given you and keep God in your life. Live life to the fullest—dream big and work toward your dreams—but be happy with whatever you have, whatever you are doing, right now. Whatever that may be. That is living life to the fullest.

You don't have to like everyone, but everyone deserves respect—and you deserve respect from everyone in return; don't accept less. Make memories you will be proud of—you can never take back actions and words that you regret—but be forgiving when you, and others, make mistakes. Be responsible, smart, and kind. Listen to your conscience; it will guide you well.

We all make mistakes, but they aren't mistakes if you learn from them. We all need advice—learn the difference between advice that is good and advice that is bad. And we all continue to learn throughout our entire lives; never assume you know it all.

Work to be fair, work to be honest. Work hard, even when you feel like giving up. And work toward peace in all that you do. Money is nice, but it won't make you happy—how you earn it and what you do with it are what matter. Earn it in a job you love and spend it on things you enjoy and people you love. Be generous. Save for a rainy day. Save for something special. Save for your future.

Find your soulmate—someone you want to be with for eternity, who feels the same way about you. Through the good times and the bad. A lifetime commitment of your hearts, like I have with your dad.

You have in your brother a true and loyal friend. Nurture this friendship. Over the years, other friendships will come and go, but this bond is deep and will last forever. Treasure it.

I believe that each of us has a purpose here on earth, something we need to do before we go on to the next great place. I believe we are here to fill with love the lives of those we touch—and I believe that that love starts at home. We give our family the gift of love, wrapped in time and patience and understanding. And then we move out from there, with more love wrapped in time and patience and understanding.

*And so do they. And then it spreads, like tufts of dandelion
fuzz riding on the wind.*

*So here you go. Drifting, blowing. Scattering goodness. Make
a good life, my sweet boy. I am so proud of you.*

Love,
Mom

My legacy in a nutshell, launched. (Or so I thought.)
Whew.

There was so much hope in that letter (times two). Hope that
first Joey and then Rick had what they needed to carry themselves
forward in all the best ways. But then the threads of our family began to unravel. Addiction. And divorce. And all the repercussions of the mess that our family has become. *All the baggage.*
Which is a kind of legacy, too, for my boys.

I've seen how Rick is judged for all the baggage that threads
its way through his roots. How Rick—the innocent bystander
through everything—is judged for having a brother with the disease of addiction, and parents who are divorced, and a dad who is
gay. That's quite a stew of stigmatized family happenings—a stew
that continues to simmer, even if on the back burner some days—
and the judgment Rick endures is not right. I wish everyone would
see Rick as the person *he* is (without looking through the lens
of who the rest of us are, first). I wish they would judge him by
how he has handled himself, with strength and compassion and
understanding—a fine example of making the best of whatever
life hands out—like he did when helping his dad to start a new
life (feeling loved), or when he soldiered on each time I abandoned
him while trying to fix and/or save Joey. Rick carries his baggage
with grace, but still, I'm sure it hurts—all of it. His parents' divorce, his broken family, his brother's addiction.

Rick,

Too often, it probably seemed like you were lost in the messy shuffle of your brother's dance with addiction, but, believe me, you weren't—at least, not in my heart. There's no question his disease changed the dynamics of our family, but this is just one more thing in the long list of things I cannot change. And I know you know I would've done everything the same way for you.

I wish I could make up for the times I was distracted or absent or crabby. I wish I could have given you a life that was more peaceful, quiet, and equal. You've never said so—you keep your feelings about this tucked away inside ten thousand boxes—but you must feel some resentment and anger. I wish I could fix that, but, just as with your brother, I know I can't and that your healing is up to you. In your own way. In your own time.

I am here to talk, to support, to aim you in the right direction if you ask. I will not harass and harangue. I do not want the toxicity of addiction to ruin what we have. All I can do is love you as you sort things out.

—*Tending Dandelions*, 196

Even though Rick is now a grown man and living far away, and even though the active chaos is now mostly behind him, my antenna is still tuned in his direction. Listening. And *hearing.* Sensing hurts that don't stop hurting just because he's an adult. Baggage. Potential storms on the horizon. Even though he can't see what's hovering about in his airwaves, I know he can feel it— and the connection, this presence, is vital.

I can't do anything about the past—all the good things and

the not-so-good things that have been done, that have happened or not happened, are *done*. And I can't do anything about what other people, any people, choose to do or think or feel or say (or *not* do or think or feel or say), or who they have become or might yet still, or whether they have (or will) learn from life's experiences in good or bad ways. But I can do more than just *wish for the best*. I can do more than just wish that our family history of *good* outweighs the *not-so-good*, that the *happy* outweighs the *not-so-happy*, and that Rick and Joey find their way to their best possible lives—wishes that also happen to be legacy-building blocks for their own generations-yet-to-come. *Yes, I can do more.*

I can be an example. Every day. With every breath.

I can set little parachutes of love and hope and positivity adrift, like dandelion seeds caught on the wind. I can choose the better path at every fork in my road, even when—especially when—I'm sad or mad or afraid (or confused, jealous, ornery). And, most importantly, I can do the right thing even when, especially when, no one seems to be looking.

I can, *I will*, honor my children with my words and my actions, living my life to its last day in the way the gift of life was meant to be lived. *This is my legacy.*

My life didn't go the way I thought it would. In fact, it went every way I thought it wouldn't. Joey's addiction, a divorce and a broken family (and broken hearts), finding a career onto which I can hang my middle-aged hat (and wallet), losing my parents to the haze of dementia, and facing old age all alone—all of these things have unraveled my world. But the only way to pull things back together is by asking myself *what for?* instead of *why me?*

And *what can I do to make things better? (Not worse.)*

For me, that means looking *inward* so I can get to a healthier place—a place from where I'll be able to carry some hope and healing *outward*. Planting seeds that might grow into something good. I know my hurts will hurt forever, but I can make them hurt less *by helping someone else to hurt less,* which, in turn, helps me to live with own my heartache and wishes.

I've seen how Joey is judged, as though addiction were a choice he made, something disgraceful or shameful even though it is *not* a moral failure on his part—or a failure on my part as his mom. Addiction is a disease, but not even the professionals have it all figured out—and they're not trying to figure it out while in a blind panic, running through the fires of hell with fears and dreams and parental instincts tripping them up—so I shouldn't feel like a total failure for not having been able to protect Joey, but still, sometimes I do.

As do countless other moms.

And so, while I wish I could also focus on raising awareness for all the other issues I've become so acutely aware of—advocacy for the elderly, mental health, and gay rights—there's only so much I can do at one time (and do well). Helping moms with addicted children—and changing the way addiction is perceived—is the battle cry I first raised, and I'm going to continue giving it my all. (But I'm present in spirit with everyone else making changes born from the pain in their lives and hearts, too.) As the mom of an addicted child, I will continue to be an ambassador of truth and understanding, changing the dynamic of the place where love and addiction meet.

My legacy, it seems, has lots of threads—I just need to see them and reach out, take hold. And *charge*.

Before my son was an addict, he was a child. My child. But he could have been anyone's child.

Before my son was an addict, he liked to fish and camp; he was an Eagle Scout and a rescue diver, and he was awarded scholarships from several colleges. He also sometimes lied and said things that were mean and sulked and was crabby; in other words, my son was perfectly normal.

There's a widely held belief that addicts are bad people, but the truth is, addiction is not an issue for moral judgment. Addiction has nothing whatsoever to do with whether a person is nice, or the quality of their character, or the strength of their will.

The word addict originates from the Latin meaning slave. So addict means: a person bound as a slave to the disease of addiction.

Addiction is a disease. Scientific research has proven this; the addicted brain exhibits measurable changes. And most addiction begins in adolescence. Our children are victims of a popular culture that strongly entices them to abuse drugs and alcohol every step of the way on their growing-up journey.

Addiction begins where dalliance—or doctors' orders— becomes disease. It can happen to anyone who has ever taken a sip or puff or snort—or even a pill prescribed for pain.

Even though my son has done some bad things while being an addict, my son is not a bad person. He's a sick person. When addiction scooped up my child, it did so indiscriminately. My son, at his core, is one of the least-bad people I know.

Before my son was an addict, I used to judge addicts very harshly. But now I know that being an addict isn't something anyone would choose. Now I know that the addict on the corner has been my sweet child.

Addiction can happen to anyone.

—from one of my presentations

When addiction is *understood* as a disease, it will be *treated* like a disease. But that's not going to happen if the world sees me, *my child's very own mom,* hiding his addiction as though it's a disgrace. So, in trading shame and blame for strength—in speaking out about the devastating truths of this disease, with my head held high—I can help people who've never lived this nightmare begin to see addiction in a different light. People might actually begin to believe that the oh-so-common word *addict* is synonymous with *someone who's sick.* (Including my son himself.)

Pain into purpose.

With *power.*

I've made a lot of progress over the past fifteen years. (Fifteen!?) So many miles and lessons and gallons of tears-like-water rushing under (and over) the bridge. My stalking and snooping, my yelling and threats and efforts to control what I can't control, are (for the most part) left in my dust. Calm (no longer crazed), educated (so not as afraid), and much more brave—now when it seems like addiction has a hold on someone I love (which, statistically, is about one loved one in ten), I speak up. Because *love* matters more than *awkward.* "I've seen things that concern me. I'm telling you this because I love you, and, even though you might just want to *shoot the messenger,* I want you to know I will be here anyway, when and if you decide you want help."

My hope is that, someday, the way the world reacts to the disease of addiction will evolve into a showing of spontaneous kindness (not madness). An understanding of who we are fighting *for* (our loved ones) and *against* (the disease consuming our loved ones). My hope is that, someday, our loved ones who need help will feel free to ask for help—without fear of judgment from their family, friends, or place of employment.

.●

Spring has sprung—in March, much earlier than last year—at least for now. The only snowflakes to be seen are in the tiny drifts clinging to shadowy corners, but it's still cold enough for a jacket—*for me*. I add that caveat because when the temperature hit a high of thirty-nine degrees the other day, I did see a couple of people wearing shorts while out walking their dogs. My neighbors are friendly, but, as bundled up as everyone was during the winter months, I'm not at all sure anymore whom I've met and whom I haven't—I've just got *tips of rosy noses* to go by for identification purposes, really. Friendly tips of noses stopping by after (or during) big snowstorms, waving at me to put my shovel away and go back inside where it's warm, as they walked up my driveway, pushing snowblowers. *Tips of noses* I'm not going to recognize as I'm outside walking again, now that all the ice has melted.

My neighborhood has an online group where everyone can connect, reaching out for things like advice on a painting project, or borrowing a tool, or announcing a sledding party. Already thinking ahead to the mowing months, I've gotten advice on gas lawn mowers to replace my electric one, which can't handle the slope of my yard—or, more accurately, I can't handle how poorly the batteries handle the slope of my yard—and I'm ready to brave using something with a gas-powered engine. It's probably still a couple of months until there's enough grass or garden growth for me to actually do any work in the yard, but my spirit is already outside playing in the dirt. I've been researching native butterfly- and bumblebee-friendly plants and am plotting out a garden in my head.

Last spring, about ten months ago, MomPower.org took flight, and it has been growing—the *sisterhood* has been growing—in leaps and bounds ever since. There's great comfort in being part of this tribe of *moms helping moms.* Moms with addicted children pulling one another up. Passing on our collective wisdom, perspective, and somewhat rickety display of sanity. Rooting for one another to make it to the other side—wherever, whatever *the other side* might be. There's great comfort in discovering the power of one among the power of many.

The power of mom power.

The power of *finding healing* in helping other moms to heal.

As moms with addicted children, we are tied together in more ways than I could ever have imagined. We are, all of us, juggling some of life's heaviest bowling balls—grief, terror, shame and guilt, helplessness and hopelessness, feelings of being all alone. We're working hard to keep two, three, four heavy burdens up in the air, sometimes even more, all at one time. But that's not all. We're also juggling the bombs that drop into our roles as moms to our other children and as wives, daughters, caregivers, worker bees, and friends. We endure the unimaginable every single day, but we have learned to cope with more things, in more ways, than we're probably even aware of. And we're doing it together— helping one another to carry the things weighing so heavily on our souls and figuring things out as we go.

You see, as moms with addicted children, we may often feel fragile, but we are strong.

And we are many.

We have the power to overpower the destruction that addiction spreads.

This—our *mom power*—is our legacy.

For the past six months, since October, I've been working on the manuscript for *Just Dandy*. Some days, the words freely fly from my heart and brain, out through my fingertips, and onto the keyboard in an unrestrained flock that can't get from *here* to *there* fast enough. Some days, the words just won't come. And some days, the words come but must be, mostly, discarded. Writing, for me, is a process of thinking and feeling and typing and deleting until what's inside comes out *just right.* When I sit in front of my laptop each morning, it's always with a bit of trepidation, knowing that *I don't know* what the day's work will churn out—hours *put in* don't guarantee pages *put out.* At the end of nine hours, I might have four good pages . . . or one pretty good paragraph. I think this is because I'm living what I'm writing about *in the now,* and things are always changing; I'm writing as I'm still sorting things out. But here I am, having made it to the last chapter. My manuscript is soon to be sent off.

Many years ago, back when I started writing a journal to collect all of my thoughts and feelings as Joey spiraled into addiction, it was an outlet (a lifeline), helping to keep me from spiraling further into the insanity that comes with being the mom of an addicted child. My journal started off as a *release.* But, in scribbling my fear- and confusion-laden words onto page after page after page, I slowly began to see things more clearly and began putting together the pieces of all my puzzled thoughts. Slowly, I discovered the healing power of putting ink to paper. And, slowly, my journal, my writing, became a scrawling strand of *change.* A way to turn pain into purpose. A way to open eyes and hearts and minds—including my own.

I've continued to write, capturing my thoughts and feelings and putting them in a safe place, as things have continued to unravel—Josh, my family as a family, my financial (in)security, and my mom and dad. I've continued to collect and untangle the threads of my story, learning and growing every step of the way. I have found new layers of courage and compassion, of integrity and forgiveness. And I've found gratitude—I've had so many years of so much happiness, and nothing, not even addiction or dementia or divorce, can take those years away.

Everything Falls Away

Sooner or later, everything falls away.
You, the work you've done, your successes,
large and small, your failures, too. Those
moments when you were light, along-
side the times you became one with the
night. The friends, the people you loved
who loved you, those who might have
wished you ill, none of this is forever. All
of it is soon to go, or going, or long gone.

Everything falls away, except the thread
you've followed, unknowing, all along.
The thread that strings together all you've
been and done, the thread you didn't know
you were tracking until, toward the end,
you see that the thread is what stays
as everything else falls away.

Follow that thread as far as you can and
you'll find that it does not end, but weaves
into the unimaginable vastness of life. Your
life never was the solo turn it seemed to be.
It was always part of the great weave of
nature and humanity, an immensity we
come to know only as we follow our own
small threads to the place where they
merge with the boundless whole.

Each of our threads runs its course, then
joins in life together. This magnificent tapestry—
this masterpiece in which we live forever.

—Parker J. Palmer

My *threads* are my legacy.

My wish is to weave them into something good.

•

I know true devastation—and I know it can fall from the sky at any time—so I've learned not to fritter away the moments I have control over with things that don't matter. Petty things. Bitter things. Stupid things. What matters is being present with my words and time and hugs while I still have the chance.

I also know the value of making peace with *it is what it is* and *whatever will be will be.* A feat, nothing short of a long, drawn-out battle. It takes *hard work* to find inner peace, which seems sort of ironic. But it's very true. And very worth it. Because without this—inner peace, carefully cultured like a pearl—whatever comes my way is harder than it needs to be.

I need to do the work so I'm prepared for whatever comes my way.

For whatever comes next.

Over the past weeks, there have been rumblings in the news about a novel virus spreading through China, then Italy, and then ravaging the population of a nursing home in Washington State. *COVID-19.* Now, all of a sudden and across the United States, schools are closing and people are working from home as the government tries to contain this thing—and so, all of a sudden, I think it's only a matter of time (a short time) before Maplewood Pointe, and therefore Mom and Dad, are locked up tight. My intuition is yelling at me to go see them *now.* When I say my goodbyes, I don't tell Mom and Dad what I'm afraid might be coming our way, but I give them each extra-big, long hugs. Just in case.

All of a sudden, again (everything seems to be happening *all of a sudden* now), Maplewood is no longer allowing visitors, including family. No one out, no one in. I'm stunned but not surprised, and I'm grateful I went to see Mom and Dad when I did, just a couple of days ago. I understand the reasoning behind the lockdown, but still, I'm having trouble comprehending the fact that I'm stuck on the outside in order to keep them safe but cannot be on the inside if—and when—they might need me the most. Or one last time. I'm having trouble comprehending the fact that I don't know when or if I'll see Mom and Dad again.

Things are happening fast—weeks are happening in days. And what's surreal is really, horribly, real.

The nurse at Maplewood Pointe calls to tell me that Mom fell earlier this morning. Because she hit her head and scraped her face, she must be taken by ambulance to the emergency room— even though their cursory exam indicates Mom is fine, and even if it means taking her from her *zone of protection* into one of the most germ-filled places of all. But, since Maplewood Pointe just implemented the lockdown yesterday, and since everything, everywhere, is, at this point, happening on the fly, they haven't had a chance to address the *risk* versus *more risk* conundrum this deadly virus presents. Thomas is already at the hospital when Mom's ambulance arrives, and within a couple of hours he's able to whisk her back to Maplewood Pointe. (He can only drop her off, passing her to an aide who will take her inside.) Mom is teetery, but okay—and probably all germed up. I won't be at all surprised if there's an outbreak over there in a few weeks and Mom is *patient zero*. With a squishiness in my stomach, I'm counting off days.

Just a week/forever ago, Thomas and I were planning on taking cupcakes and gifts over to Maplewood Pointe to celebrate Mom's ninety-third birthday with her and Dad. Instead, now, with things as they are, Nurse Patricia and I tag-team a birthday video chat with Mom. (Standing outside the window and waving—as some awesome people are doing with their own locked-up elders—won't work with Mom since she lives on the third floor and won't talk on the phone. On top of the confusion of *dementia*.) For our call, I wear the unicorn headband that Mom should be wearing—a cheerful extravaganza of silver lamé, a rainbow of brightly colored tulle, and fuchsia glitter—a headband I'd bought so she could trot happily up and down her hall in full regalia. Mom laughs at the spectacle. We talk for only a few minutes; she is perplexed by my rectangular presence in Patricia's palm, but I expected that. I sing Mom a quick and croaky verse of "Happy Birthday" and tell her she looks great (and really, the scrapes and bruise on her face don't look too bad). She replies by saying she needs to be laid out on *one of those boards* so all her wrinkles can be ironed out. After blowing kisses and hanging up, I wear the headband around the house for the rest of the morning.

Sometime after moving Mom and Dad from their marital home into the place they live now—Dad on the assisted-living side of the expansive brick building and Mom behind the locked doors of memory care down the hall—I became aware of something I had somehow never been aware of before: Dad doesn't complain. About anything. Ever. Not about the myriad (and drastic) changes that have taken over (and keep taking over) his life, and not about anything else, as far back as I can remember. Never once. He talks about things, of course—he's not all *lalalala* and rose-colored glasses—but he talks about things very matter-of-factly. Observationally. Stoically. Even now that he's locked away and stuck inside. He accepts what is. And he is content.

Dad sort of understands what's going on with this unfolding pandemic: *there's a bug going around they don't want us to catch.* But then he sort of forgets. He knows I can't visit, but then wonders if I'd like to take him out for lunch tomorrow; it hurts my heart to have to remind him over and over that I can't see him for a while (*but hopefully soon, Dad!*). And he knows he can't go outside for his daily walks—he says when he peeks out the front door (at what used to be his gateway to freedom), there's a sign to remind him. But, when I talked to him earlier today, he'd been getting ready to head outside and enjoy this fine spring day. Dad talks about the outdoors with such wistfulness; it's a real possibility that one of these days he will accidentally slip out and won't be allowed back in.

The dining room is closed; meals are now delivered to the residents' apartments, so everyone is eating alone. Activities are suspended. And when Dad walks the halls, there's no one out and about for him to even wave and smile at. Socializing, even if anyone else were out in the halls, is not allowed. The only people Dad sees day after day (and forever now, it seems) are the aides who deliver his meals, and Mom—whom, for now, he's still permitted to visit. None of the new social distancing procedures really affect Mom; she's been happily living the recluse life for a long time. But if and when the time comes that Dad can no longer walk down the hall to see her four or five times every day, I truly don't know how either of them will survive.

Thomas, Jonathan, and I are each making phone calls to Dad every day—he's no longer able to use his computer or cell phone, but FaceTime probably would have been too much to handle anyway, so this is the only way we have to connect. As *connect* goes, these days. We're sending happy things in the mail and dropping care packages off at the front door, things he can look at again and again. We're trying to fill his days, now full of *nothing,* with *something.* And we're hoping he will remember to pass the *little somethings* on to Mom—that is our only (and wishful) way to connect with her.

Every time I call Dad, I begin by asking, "How are you doing today, Big Daddy?" Or Pops, depending on the day. And every time, he replies in the same way he has for years:

Just perfect!

But with each passing week, Dad's voice is fading.

Just perfect!

Just perfect!

The isolation is, already, slowly sucking the life out of Dad. *I can hear it.* Thinking of him, Mom, and everyone else's parents who are living out their last bit of life so lonely, without hugs, without the gift of touch, breaks my heart. It's very possible that Mom and Dad might die alone, with none of us children there to hold their hands. I trust, because I must, that the people taking care of them are doing their very best.

Rick has been working from home for the past few weeks, and I've been trying to convince him to do his work from here, at my home in Minnesota, or at his dad's house on the beach. I want him to get out of New York City, the hot spot of the coronavirus, where all hell is breaking loose. (And, to be honest, since I haven't seen another human being in person since giving my parents their last hugs, it would just be nice to have him around.) But his roommate has been coughing all of a sudden, and Rick doesn't want to go anywhere till he's sure he's not contagious. I am so proud of him, of his ethics . . . but, oh my gosh, I wish he could just GO. I tell Rick to stock up on groceries and to wash his hands (a lot), and I send him a copy of my living will, just in case. I remind him that I don't want to live as *long* as I can—there's a big difference between life span and health span, and I'm not afraid of going on to the next place.

Joey has lost his job and is planning to sail the boat he lives on, which he doesn't know how to sail, from Florida to New York—into the fire.

More than ever, with everyone I love, I need to find ways to be together while apart.

I knew it was only a matter of time before Josh would contact me about alimony; I just didn't think he would try to dump me so quickly. Or completely. But that's what happened today, just a few weeks into this pandemic. He's done. *I cannot pay alimony until I have a better idea of where and how this virus will affect my income . . . sorry I can't send money, hopefully is a temporary issue.* Not even a *good luck.* Even though alimony is a legal obligation and, without it, I have no way to pay my bills. And, of course, there are no jobs to be had right now. All of my fears, the vulnerabilities of being alone, are suddenly even more real. I'm trying to wrap my head and heart around all of this. I'm trying to comprehend the devastation caused by Josh's violent tug on my rug.

March 2020. Nothing, absolutely nothing, is in my control. Nothing, except *me.* But I've been in training for this for years. I have control over *how I react* to the things I have no control over. I have the power to make things better, not worse, and I will move forward, trying to make things better however I can. The wild ride of the pandemic—and it's only just begun—has made it very clear how important it is to keep working on myself. So I can focus on what really matters. My legacy. And living right.

> *It's easy to forget, in the hubbub of life, that my purpose here is to make—and leave—the world a better place. No matter what happens around me.*
>
> *My purpose doesn't have to be grand or showy. It can be simple. And quiet. And shuffle along like a tortoise, one slow-and-steady day at a time. I can take my unique talents, whatever they may be, and use them to touch one person at a time, or to touch a whole crowd of people. No matter how*

I proceed, I will make an impact. My hands and feet and motherly arms have a purpose to fulfill that is bigger than me. I don't need any credit; no one even has to know what I do.

We are born. We die. In between those two momentous occasions we have the potential to make and leave the world a better place: the purpose of purpose.

One day, one choice.

I vow that my time here on earth will not be wasted.

—Tending Dandelions, 223

The Plan: Just Dandy

(while living with heartache and wishes)

HERE ARE FOUR SIMPLE STEPS to help you move forward in positive ways (instead of getting lost in the turmoil of life, which is so easy to do):

1. Start each day with a kind word or two to yourself.

2. Start each day with the goal of doing at least one thing to help yourself become your best self possible, whatever that may be, whatever you feel up to—big or small, personal or out-reaching—on any given day.

3. Start each day by jotting down the kind words you said to yourself and the thing you want to get done—because jotting things down helps make them real.

4. Finish each day by reading the nice thing you said to yourself when you started your day and then cross off your day's goal—the thing you did to help yourself become the best *you* possible—and enjoy feeling good that you did it.

Every day is a new day. Every day is a chance to bloom anew.

About the Author

Sandra Swenson is the mother of two sons—one of whom struggles with addiction. Author of the books *The Joey Song: A Mother's Story of Her Son's Addiction* and *Tending Dandelions: Honest Meditations for Mothers with Addicted Children* and the *Readings for Moms of Addicts* app, Sandra lives in the place where love and addiction meet—a place where help enables and hope hurts. Sandra is a voice for parents of children suffering with the disease of addiction, putting their thoughts and feeling into words. Her latest project is MomPower.org, an easy-to-navigate hub connecting moms who have children with addictions to a world of help, hope, perspective, sanity, and empowerment.

Sandra lives in suburban Minneapolis, Minnesota. When she isn't writing or traveling to speak with other parents who are coping with the disease of addiction in their families, Sandra enjoys gardening, reading, and spending time with family and friends.

About Hazelden Publishing

As part of the Hazelden Betty Ford Foundation, Hazelden Publishing offers both cutting-edge educational resources and inspirational books. Our print and digital works help guide individuals in treatment and recovery, and their loved ones. Professionals who work to prevent and treat addiction also turn to Hazelden Publishing for evidence-based curricula, digital content solutions, and videos for use in schools, treatment and correctional programs, and community settings. We also offer training for implementation of our curricula.

Through published and digital works, Hazelden Publishing extends the reach of healing and hope to individuals, families, and communities affected by addiction and related issues.

For more information about Hazelden publications,
please call **800-328-9000**
or visit us online at **hazelden.org/bookstore**.

Other Titles That May Interest You

Without Shame
The Addict's Mom and Her Family Share Their Stories of Pain and Healing
BARBARA THEODOSIOU
In *Without Shame*, Barbara Theodosiou and her family reveal the pain, loss, and connection that emerge from addiction, trauma, codependency, and recovery in this unique view into the heart of a national crisis.
Order No. 3561; also available as an ebook

Living Without Shame
A Support Book for Mothers with Addicted Children
BARBARA THEODOSIOU
Living Without Shame is the follow-up support book to Barbara Theodosiou's family account of addiction, *Without Shame*. Recipient of a White House Champion of Change award, Theodosiou continues to help other mothers of addicted children with this interactive healing journal for moms.
Order No. 3562

Find Your Light
Practicing Mindfulness to Recover from Anything
BEVERLY CONYERS
Author Beverly Conyers—a respected voice in recovery and wellness—has guided hundreds of thousands of readers through the process of recognizing, treating, and healing from addiction. With her newest work, Conyers shows us how the practice of mindfulness can be a game-changing part of recovering from anything and everything.
Order No. 3591; also available as an ebook

Hazelden books are available at fine bookstores everywhere.
To order directly from Hazelden, call **800-328-9000**
or visit **hazelden.org/bookstore**.

Other Titles by Sandra Swenson

Tending Dandelions
Honest Meditations for Mothers of Addicted Children
These meditations provide encouragement and understanding for moms who are realizing that recovery rarely follows a neat or comfortable path. By sharing the experiences that are unique to families facing addiction, *Tending Dandelions* offers wisdom, support, and inspiration for the recovery journey.
Order No. 3481; also available as an ebook

The Joey Song
A Mother's Story of Her Son's Addiction
The Joey Song is the poignant story of a defiant addict and the mother who won't give up on him. She finally realizes that it hurts more to hang on than to let go, and that letting go is not the same thing as giving up. Sandra Swenson beautifully orchestrates a mother's lessons of love and loss while surviving her son's addiction.
Order No. 3564; also available as an ebook

Readings for Moms of Addicts
This mobile app, available for Apple or Android devices, contains 146 readings that are different from, yet complementary to, the meditations in *Tending Dandelions.* This convenient and searchable app format provides the perfect tool for use in support groups—such as Al-Anon, Nar-Anon Family Groups, or Families Anonymous—or at any time you need connection and motivation.
Order No. AP3481 for the Apple app and AA3481 for the Android app

Hazelden books are available at fine bookstores everywhere.
To order directly from Hazelden, call **800-328-9000**
or visit **hazelden.org/bookstore.**